Court TRANSCRIPTS

A WINDOW ON THE CRIMINAL JUSTICE SYSTEM

Second Edition

Deborah Klein
Attorney at Law
College of DuPage

Kendall Hunt
publishing company

Cover images © Shutterstock, Inc.

Kendall Hunt
publishing company
www.kendallhunt.com
Send all inquiries to:
4050 Westmark Drive
Dubuque, IA 52004-1840

ISBN 978-1-4652-2082-0

Printed in the United States of America
10 9 8 7 6 5 4 3 2 1

Contents

Preface

Having served more than a decade in the courtroom representing the government in the role of prosecuting attorney, I developed a great respect for the law and the criminal justice system. I loved the engagement of criminal court proceedings. Now as a Professor of Criminal Justice, I find it impractical to bring students to the courtroom as often as I would like, so instead, I try to bring the courtroom to the students. Towards that end, I have developed the following transcripts to afford students an opportunity to view how the concepts presented in their criminal justice textbooks may play out in an actual courtroom. I believe these transcripts can enhance, in a realistic way, a student's understanding of the role of law enforcement and how our adversarial system operates.

This text is designed to serve either as a supplement to a criminal justice textbook or as a stand-alone text. Each of five parts represents a different area within the criminal court system. The list of key terms highlights what is addressed in each Part. Applicable Illinois statutes have been included for reference. The transcript format allows for ease in location of specific points for classroom discussion. The short-answer exercises, whether completed in class or turned in as assignments, provide an easy check of student assessment. Classroom students may even wish to role-play the trials contained in Part III.

Although the transcripts are intended to realistically portray criminal justice proceedings, the names and places contained within are fictitious. Welcome to Columbia County, Illinois!

Professor Deborah Klein
College of DuPage
Attorney at Law

PART I

INITIAL STAGES: FELONY

KEY TERMS		
adversarial system	felony	plea
arraignment	grand jury	preliminary hearing
arrest	indictment	probable cause
bond	information	release on recognizance
complaint	initial appearance	speedy trial
constitutional rights	jurisdiction	true bill
courtroom work group	*Miranda* warnings	warrant

INTRODUCTION

People v. Crude

In the early morning hours on July 3, Macy Morgan walks into the Columbia City Police Department. Macy reports to Officer Jack Friendly that she has been raped, her residence has been broken into, and property has been taken. Macy has unwittingly entered the criminal justice system. Officer Friendly is just hours away from placing Max Crude under arrest. Max, too, will enter the criminal justice system. You may review Officer Friendly's initial report as he begins his investigation. You may read for yourself what transpires in the courtroom when Max Crude has his initial appearance before a judge, appears for his preliminary hearing, and is subsequently arraigned on the charges of Criminal Sexual Assault, Residential Burglary, and Theft.

People v. Berry

Later on July 3, Officer Friendly testifies before a grand jury, where he relates how he located heroin in the possession of Rex Berry following a routine search conducted after arresting Berry on an out of county warrant. You may read the transcript of the officer's testimony before the grand jury, review the Indictment prepared by the State's Attorney's Office, and review the true bill signed by the foreperson of the grand jury, as well as the arrest warrant for the new felony charge.

ARREST REPORT

Officer Friendly initiated an investigation into the allegations made by Morgan and a case number has been assigned. Appearing in the next pages is the Officer's completed Arrest Report and his initial narrative report. As the investigation continues, supplements will be made to the report.

INITIAL APPEARANCE

Illinois law requires that once a person is arrested, that person is to be taken "without unnecessary delay" before a judge in the county where the arrest occurred. The appearance may be in person or, if the defendant is in custody, the hearing may be conducted via closed circuit television. The judge must inform the defendant of the charge or charges against him (providing a copy of the charging document) and advise the defendant of his right to counsel. When appropriate, the judge will schedule a preliminary hearing as well as address the issue of bond.

PRELIMINARY HEARING

In Illinois, a defendant charged with a felony offense will receive a preliminary hearing within 30 days from the date they were taken into custody. At such hearing, the judge will determine from the evidence whether it appears there is probable cause to believe the offense was committed by the defendant. The prosecutor carries the burden of proof at this hearing. If the judge determines probable cause does not exist to believe the defendant guilty of any offense, the charge will be dismissed.

The defendant has the option of waiving, or giving up, his right to a preliminary hearing. By waiving the preliminary hearing, the prosecutor need not present evidence and the defendant will be held to answer to the pending charge or charges.

ARRAIGNMENT

Following waiver, or a finding of probable cause at the preliminary hearing, the defendant will appear for an arraignment before the judge with jurisdiction over the case. The defendant will again be informed of the charge or charges against him, but for the first time will be asked to enter a plea. Most defendants enter a plea of not guilty at this stage, whereupon a trial date will be set. The Illinois speedy trial law requires the trial date be set within 120 days from arrest if the defendant is in custody.

GRAND JURY

In Illinois, the State's Attorney has the option of filing a criminal complaint charging an individual with an offense or seeking an Indictment from a grand jury. A grand jury consists of 16 persons, one of which is selected to serve as foreperson. The foreperson presides over the hearings and swears all witnesses. The grand jury hears evidence presented by the State's Attorney. If a sufficient number of grand jurors agree that the evidence demonstrates probable cause to believe a person has committed an offense, the State's Attorney will prepare a Bill of Indictment charging that person with the offense; the Indictment is then signed by the foreperson.

Grand jury proceedings differ from virtually all other proceedings in our criminal justice system in that the sessions are held in strict secrecy, outside the presence of a judge, defense counsel, or defendant. Generally, only the State's Attorney, a court reporter, and the witness testifying at the time are present as evidence is presented to the grand jurors. A court may order that the Indictment be kept secret until the defendant is in custody.

COLUMBIA CITY POLICE
ARREST REPORT

Case No. **CPD00759-14** **Arrest Date** **07-03-14**

Name of person arrested: (enter on line below) Alias:
Max Crude

Address of suspect:	City:	State:
123 E. Front Street	Columbia City	IL

SSN:	Age:	Race:	Sex:	Eyes:	Hair:
555-00-1212	25	Caucasian	M	Brown	Brown

Ht.	Wt.	DOB:	Place of Birth:
6'0"	190	05-12-89	Columbia City, IL

Location of arrest:	Time of arrest:
123 E. Front Street (residence)	06:05

Where offense committed:	Date:	Time:
10 Center St. (parking lot)	07-02-14	approx. 24:00

Circle all that apply:
Armed: No Yes-weapon ______________ Drunk Drinking Resisted Cursed

Vehicle Involved:
Year 2012 Make Ford Model Fusion Color white License # 689 0578 State IL

Name of Complainant:	DOB:	Relationship (if any)
Macy Morgan	07-01-93	friend

Address of Complainant:	Home phone:
29 Water St.	100-455-2318

City, State:	Work phone:
Columbia City, IL	100-232-5554

Name and address of witness(es):
Sandra Gates, 9424 17th Street, Columbia City, IL

Offense(s) suspected or charged:	Statute:
Criminal Sexual Assault	720 ILCS 5/11-1.20

Arresting officer(s): J. Friendly (Badge #143)
Report made by: J. Friendly (Badge #143)

NARRATIVE REPORT Case No: CPD00759-14

At 04:00 on July 3, 2014, Macy Morgan appeared at CPD along with her friend Sandra Gates, indicating she wished to speak to an officer. I, J. Friendly (Badge #143) met with Morgan in an interview room while Gates waited in the reception area. Morgan appeared quite shaken. Morgan related that about one month ago, she started messaging 25-year-old Max Crude whom she had met through an online dating service. The first time they had met in person was the night before reporting to the police. Crude told Morgan he wanted to take her out to celebrate the fact that she had just turned 21.

Morgan further reported that Crude picked her up at her residence at approximately 20:00 on July 2. They drove directly to Jody's Bar & Grill in Columbia City. Morgan and Crude drank a couple pitchers of beer, and each had a couple shots of tequila. Crude and Morgan spent a lot of time discussing music genres and both liked acid blues. Morgan thought things were going well between them when Crude said he would like to listen to her extensive collection of vinyl albums from the '60s and '70s.

At 24:00, Morgan told Crude she was not feeling well. Crude helped Morgan out to his car and got into the backseat with her. Crude told Morgan, "I know what will make you feel better." Morgan said Crude then started kissing her, removed her pants, and penetrated her vagina with his penis. Morgan stated she remembers saying "no" and tried to push him away, but she doesn't remember much. The next thing Morgan knew, she woke up lying in the parking lot of Jody's Bar. Crude was gone. After locating her phone, Morgan called her friend Gates for a ride home. Morgan and Gates arrived at Morgan's residence about 03:00. Morgan found that the back door of the residence had been kicked open and her entire collection of vinyl albums, which Morgan feels are worth in excess of $500, was gone.

Morgan stated she had not showered or urinated since leaving Jody's parking lot. I asked Morgan to respond to the Emergency Room at the Central Columbia Hospital. Morgan indicated she would have Gates take her there right away. Morgan and Gates agreed to come back to the station later in the day to complete written statements.

I followed Gates and Morgan to the hospital. Once in the ER, I informed the nurse on duty, Sophia Morris, of my investigation and asked that a sex crime kit be completed on Morgan. Following the examination of Morgan, Morris indicated she observed bruising on Morgan's right hip and right elbow. Semen was detected in Morgan's vagina. Morris indicated the lack of additional trauma did not preclude that a rape had occurred. I obtained the sex crime kit from Morris and took it back to the department where it was properly secured in evidence for further testing.

A computer check on Crude revealed a juvenile record but no adult criminal history. At 06:00, I responded to Crude's residence in Columbia City. Crude identified himself. I informed Crude that Morgan had reported an incident from the previous night. I asked Crude if he wished to give me his side of the story. Crude indicated he had nothing to tell me. I informed Crude he was under arrest for felony Criminal Sexual Assault and other charges would be pending. Crude was transported to the Columbia County Jail.

ARREST REPORT EXERCISE

NAME ____

COURSE ____

DATE ____

Please provide full and complete responses to the following five questions:

1. The arrest report completed by the officer contains very detailed information. What reasons can you think of for requiring this amount of detail? Who will be reading this report?

2. What is required for an officer to make a lawful arrest? What facts could the officer rely upon at the time the arrest was made? Was the arrest lawful? State your reasoning.

3. The narrative report does not state that the suspect was *Mirandized* at the time of his arrest or during transport to the jail. Assume *Miranda* was not given. Under these circumstances, is that a violation of the arrestee's Fifth Amendment right? Explain.

4. According to the narrative report, the officer placed the suspect under arrest on the charge of Criminal Sexual Assault (rape) and stated other charges would be pending. To what charges could the officer have been referring? Does probable cause exist for these charges? Explain.

5. Once the suspect was placed under arrest, what types of searches could the officer lawfully conduct? Explain.

The defendant has been arrested and charged with the felony offenses of Criminal Sexual Assault, Residential Burglary, and Theft. The following is a transcript from the defendant's initial appearance

ONCE COURT CONVENED, THE FOLLOWING TOOK PLACE:

PRESENT: JUDGE
CLERK
BAILIFF
DEFENDANT

BAILIFF: All rise, court is now in session.

THE COURT: Please be seated. Would the clerk please call the first case on today's docket?

CLERK: *People v. Crude*, defendant Max Crude.

THE COURT: Bailiff, please bring the defendant forward. Is your name Max Crude?

DEFENDANT: Yes, Your Honor.

THE COURT: Bailiff, please hand to Mr. Crude a copy of the Complaint filed by the State's Attorney's Office in this matter. Mr. Crude, is that your date of birth that appears on the document you have just been handed?

DEFENDANT: Yes Sir, it is.

THE COURT: You have been charged with the felony offenses of criminal Sexual Assault, Residential Burglary, and Theft. Mr. Crude, do you wish for me to read the Complaint to you?

DEFENDANT: No Sir, that is not necessary.

THE COURT: Mr. Crude, these are very serious charges for which you could be sentenced to prison. Do you have counsel?

DEFENDANT: No, Your Honor, I cannot afford to retain a lawyer. I completed an application for a public defender to represent me.

THE COURT: Very well. Allow me to review your application. I see that you are employed full time.

DEFENDANT: Yes Sir. I just started this job last month.

THE COURT: You have no savings? No assets?

DEFENDANT: I have no money saved. I have a car that I am making payments on and a computer. That is about it.

THE COURT: Is there anyone from whom you could borrow money to retain counsel?

DEFENDANT: No, Your Honor, I do not know anyone with that kind of money.

THE COURT: Very well. I consider you indigent and will appoint the Public Defender's Office to represent you. You will be given an appointment to meet with the public defender assigned to represent you should you post bond. If you cannot post bond, the public defender will meet with you at the jail.

THE COURT: Your bond has been set at $100,000. I am going to continue that bond. Furthermore, I am ordering that you not have contact, either directly or indirectly, with the complainant in this case.

DEFENDANT: Your Honor, if I do not show up for work tomorrow, I will be fired. Could I be released on my own recognizance?

THE COURT: No, I do not believe that would be appropriate given the serious nature of these charges. You may discuss the issue of bond with the public defender. Your attorney may schedule a Bond Reduction Hearing or address the issue of bond at a later time.

DEFENDANT: Thank you.

THE COURT: Since you have been arrested and charged with felony offenses, you are entitled by State law to receive either a preliminary examination or an indictment by Grand Jury within 30 days from the date you were taken into custody. I am going to schedule a preliminary hearing for two weeks from today. If you are unable to post bond, you will be transported from the jail for that hearing.

DEFENDANT: Yes Sir.

THE COURT: Do you have any questions for me at this time?

DEFENDANT: No.

THE COURT: If there is nothing further Mr. Crude, you will be escorted back to the jail.

INITIAL APPEARANCE EXERCISE

NAME ____

COURSE ____

DATE ____

Please provide full and complete responses to the following five questions:

1. The defendant appears on his charges in State court. The crimes occurred in Columbia County. What does that information tell you about the location of the court? How do you know?

2. Which amendment provides for the assistance of counsel? Is the defendant automatically entitled to have counsel appointed to represent him on these felony offenses? What does the judge mean by "indigent"?

3. The judge scheduled a preliminary hearing. If the defendant were in Federal court, would he have a preliminary hearing? Explain.

4. The defendant asked to be released on his own recognizance (ROR). What is he asking of the judge? What factors would the judge have considered in denying the defendant's request for ROR? Does the bond amount seem appropriate? Why or why not?

5. The defendant was booked into jail for one offense, yet is now charged with three felony offenses. Who filed those charges? The judge did not ask the defendant to enter a plea to these felony offenses. How does this differ from misdemeanor court?

The defendant has been arrested and charged with the felony offenses of Criminal Sexual Assault, Residential Burglary, and Theft. The defendant has had his initial appearance before a judge and is now back in court for his preliminary hearing. The following is a transcript from the defendant's preliminary hearing.

ONCE COURT CONVENED, THE FOLLOWING TOOK PLACE:

PRESENT: JUDGE
CLERK
BAILIFF
ASSISTANT STATE'S ATTORNEY
PUBLIC DEFENDER
DEFENDANT

THE COURT: We will now take up the matter of *People v. Crude,* which is scheduled for preliminary hearing today. Mr. Crude, I see that you have been brought over from the jail for today's hearing and that you are represented by the Public Defender's Office.

DEFENDANT: Yes Sir.

THE COURT: You are entitled to receive a preliminary examination on the felony charges of Criminal Sexual Assault, Residential Burglary, and Theft with which you have been charged. Do you understand the purpose of today's hearing, Mr. Crude?

DEFENDANT: Yes, I think so.

THE COURT: The prosecution has the burden of establishing that the crimes with which you have been charged were committed, and that you, Mr. Crude, probably committed those crimes. Have you discussed this matter with your attorney?

DEFENDANT: Yes, Your Honor.

THE COURT: You may exercise your right to have the prosecutor present evidence. If from the evidence it appears there is probable cause to believe you have committed the offenses, you shall be held to answer to the court. If the prosecution does not meet its burden on a particular charge, I will dismiss that charge. Do you understand?

DEFENDANT: Yes, Your Honor.

THE COURT: You also have the right to waive, or give up, your right to this hearing. If you waive the hearing, your case will be transferred to another court where you will be asked to enter a plea. If you enter a plea of not guilty, a trial date will be set. Is that clear?

DEFENDANT: Yes, Your Honor.

THE COURT: How does the defense wish to proceed?

PUBLIC DEFENDER: Your Honor, I have had an opportunity to discuss this case with Mr. Crude and with the Assistant State's Attorney. Mr. Crude wishes to waive his preliminary hearing.

THE COURT: Very well. Based upon your waiver, I find that probable cause exists that the felony offenses of Criminal Sexual Assault, Residential Burglary, and Theft were committed and that the defendant probably committed those crimes. Mr. Crude, your case will be assigned to another court where you will appear next Monday. Your attorney will provide you with the details.

PUBLIC DEFENDER: Your Honor, the defense would like to be heard on the issue of bond.

THE COURT: Proceed.

PUBLIC DEFENDER: Mr. Crude has resided in this county all of his life. He has family here, he has a job, and he assures me he will be present for all future court dates.

THE COURT: Does the defendant have a criminal history?

ASSISTANT STATE'S ATTORNEY: No, Your Honor. A computer check reveals no prior arrests or convictions as an adult.

PUBLIC DEFENDER: Your Honor, my client is indigent and cannot post bond of $100,000. I am asking the Court to release my client on his own recognizance, or in the alternative, if the Court feels there must be a bond posted, that bond be reduced to $10,000, an amount his family can post for him.

THE COURT: What is the position of the People?

ASSISTANT STATE'S ATTORNEY: We feel a release on recognizance would be inappropriate given the charges. We are not opposed to a reduction in the bond. We would leave the amount in the discretion of the court.

THE COURT: Considering argument of counsel for the defendant and the Assistant State's Attorney, I will reduce the bond to $10,000. Should you post bond, Mr. Crude, you must promise to remain within the State and appear for all scheduled hearings. I will continue the condition that you have no contact with the complainant. You will now be returned to the jail pending posting of the bond.

PRELIMINARY HEARING EXERCISE

NAME ____

COURSE ____

DATE ____

Please provide full and complete responses to the following five questions:

1. What members of the courtroom work group are present at the defendant's preliminary hearing? Is there anyone present who is not a member of this group?

2. U.S. trial courts operate under what is known as the adversarial system. Explain what that term means.

3. Explain the purpose of a preliminary hearing. Who has the burden of proof? What is the role of the judge at this hearing?

4. Is it necessary for defense counsel to believe their client is innocent? What is the role of defense counsel? Who is better able to provide a defense for a criminal defendant—a public defender or private counsel? State your reasoning.

5. How does a preliminary hearing differ from a grand jury proceeding? How does a preliminary hearing differ from a jury trial?

At the preliminary hearing, the defendant was bound over to Circuit Court to answer to the charges of Criminal Sexual Assault, Residential Burglary, and Theft. The following is a transcript from the defendant's arraignment in Circuit Court.

ONCE COURT CONVENED, THE FOLLOWING TOOK PLACE:

PRESENT: JUDGE
CLERK
BAILIFF
ASSISTANT STATE'S ATTORNEY
PUBLIC DEFENDER
DEFENDANT

THE COURT: Would the clerk please call the next case?

CLERK: *People v. Crude.* The defendant, Max Crude, appears for arraignment.

THE COURT: Counsel, you are present with your client, Max Crude?

PUBLIC DEFENDER: Yes, Your Honor.

THE COURT: Bailiff, please hand to the defendant a copy of the Information. Counsel, does your client wish to have the charges read to him?

PUBLIC DEFENDER: No, Your Honor. I reviewed the charges with my client prior to court today.

THE COURT: Very well. Before I ask you to enter a plea, Mr. Crude, I want to make sure you are aware of certain Constitutional rights that you have. You have already exercised your Sixth Amendment right to have an attorney appointed to represent you in this matter. The right to counsel extends even beyond the trial. Have you had ample time to discuss the case with your attorney so that you feel comfortable in entering a plea today?

DEFENDANT: Yes, Your Honor.

THE COURT: You have a Fifth Amendment right against self-incrimination. That means if you have a trial on these charges, the prosecutor cannot call you as a witness or otherwise compel you to take the stand. Do you understand that right?

DEFENDANT: Yes, Your Honor.

THE COURT: The Sixth Amendment affords you the right to a speedy trial. In this State, that means you must be tried within 160 days from the date you request a trial. If you were still in custody, you would have to be tried within 120 days from the date you were arrested. Do you understand your right to a speedy trial?

DEFENDANT: Yes, Your Honor.

THE COURT: You have the right to a trial by jury, or you may waive that right in open court. Have you discussed this right with your attorney?

DEFENDANT: I have Your Honor.

THE COURT: You have additional rights under the Sixth Amendment. At a trial, you would have the right to compel witnesses on your behalf. That means you may subpoena witnesses to appear at trial and testify. Through your attorney, you would also have the right to cross-examine witnesses called by the prosecution. Do you understand these rights?

DEFENDANT: I do Your Honor.

THE COURT: Very well. According to State law, you may now enter a plea of guilty, guilty but mentally ill, or not guilty. Should you stand mute, a plea of not guilty will be entered for you, and a trial will be set. How do you plead?

DEFENDANT: Not guilty.

PUBLIC DEFENDER: My client demands a jury trial.

THE COURT: Very well. Will the clerk please check the court's calendar for a trial date?

CLERK: Four months from today, Judge.

THE COURT: Is that date acceptable, counsel?

ASSISTANT STATE'S ATTORNEY: Yes, Judge, we will be ready.

PUBLIC DEFENDER: That is fine.

THE COURT: I see, Mr. Crude, that you have posted bond in this case. I will continue that bond with the conditions previously imposed. If there are no questions, then court will be in recess.

BAILIFF: All rise.

ARRAIGNMENT AND PLEA EXERCISE

NAME ______________________________

COURSE ______________________________

DATE ______________________________

Please provide full and complete responses to the following five questions:

1. At what stage in the trial process does the arraignment occur? What is the purpose of the arraignment?

2. The judge advised the defendant of certain Constitutional rights he possesses. What rights did the judge mention under the Sixth Amendment? What about the Fifth Amendment?

3. What appears to be the role of the bailiff in the courtroom?

4. List and explain the various pleas a criminal defendant may enter to a charge.

5. The judge specifically mentioned the defendant's right to a speedy trial. Why is this an important right? Why would the State provide different time periods for speedy trial? Does four months from the time of arraignment until trial seem "speedy" to you? Explain.

A proposed bill of indictment is before the Grand Jury. The State's Attorney's Office will present evidence on the count of Unlawful Possession of a Controlled Substance, Heroin. The following is a transcript from a portion of the day's proceedings.

PRESENT: GRAND JURY FOREPERSON
14 GRAND JURORS
ASSISTANT STATE'S ATTORNEY
WITNESS – OFFICER
WITNESS – EVIDENCE TECHNICIAN

ASSISTANT STATE'S ATTORNEY: Going on the record, this is *The People of the State of Illinois v. Rex Berry.*

The proposed bill of indictment states that on or about July 2, 2014, in said Columbia County, State of Illinois, Rex Berry committed the offense of unlawful possession of a controlled substance, in that he did knowingly and unlawfully have in his possession less than 15 grams of a substance containing a controlled substance, heroin, in violation of Chapter 720, Act 570, Section 401(c) of the Illinois Compiled Statutes.

The Grand Jury has the right to subpoena and question any person against whom the State's Attorney is seeking a bill of indictment or any other person, and to obtain and examine any documents or transcripts relevant to the matter being prosecuted by the State's Attorney.

JACK FRIENDLY, a witness called on behalf of the People, being first duly sworn in front of the Grand Jury, was examined and testified as follows:

EXAMINATION OF WITNESS

ASSISTANT STATE'S ATTORNEY: Please state your name and occupation for the Grand Jury.

A: My name is Jack Friendly. I work as a police officer.

Q: In your capacity as a police officer, did you place an individual by the name of Rex Berry under arrest on July 2, 2014?

A: Yes I did.

Q: Please tell the Grand Jury your involvement in the arrest of Rex Berry.

A: I went to Mr. Berry's residence to arrest him on a felony warrant issued by another county.

Q: What did you do once you arrived at the residence?

A: I knocked on the door. I confirmed that the individual who answered was Rex Berry. I informed Mr. Berry of the warrant and placed him under arrest.

Q: What did you do next?

A: After conducting a pat down for weapons, I transported Mr. Berry to the county jail for booking.

Q: Then what happened?

A: I escorted Mr. Berry into the booking area of the jail and removed his cuffs. I then conducted a more thorough search of his person. I checked his shoes and socks. When I checked his mouth, I found a small baggie containing a white substance. I told him to spit it out.

Q: What did you do with this baggie?

A: I tested the contents using a standard field test kit. The contents tested positive for heroin.

Q: Then what happened?

A: The correctional officer began the booking process on the out-of-county warrant. I turned the baggie and the remaining contents over to the evidence technician once I got back to the department.

ASSISTANT STATE'S ATTORNEY: Do any of the Grand Jurors have questions for this witness? [No audible response.]

ASSISTANT STATE'S ATTORNEY: Okay. Officer, you may step down.

PAT PERKINS, a witness called on behalf of the People being first duly sworn in front of the Grand Jury, was examined and testified as follows:

EXAMINATION OF WITNESS

ASSISTANT STATE'S ATTORNEY: Please state your name and occupation for the Grand Jury.

A: My name is Pat Perkins. I work for the City as an evidence technician in the police department.

Q: Are you a sworn peace officer?

A: No, I am not. I am a civilian employee.

Q: Were you working on July 2, 2014?

A: Yes I was.

Q: Did you receive into evidence that day a baggie containing a white substance from Officer Friendly?

A: Yes I did.

Q: Was that baggie and its contents attributable to Rex Berry?

A: Yes.

Q: What has been done with that baggie and its contents since Officer Friendly turned it over to you on that date?

A: It was logged into our system, sealed, and placed into a secure locker to which only evidence personnel have access. The next day I removed the baggie and its contents, packaged it, and sent it to the crime lab for testing. I subsequently received the baggie and its remaining contents, along with a certified report from the crime lab indicating the substance tested positive for heroin.
I placed the sealed baggie back into a secure locker where it remains.

ASSISTANT STATE'S ATTORNEY: Do any of the Grand Jurors have questions for this witness?

GRAND JUROR #12: Yes. Where is the report now?

WITNESS: I brought it with me to the Courthouse.

GRAND JUROR #12: Can we please see that document?

ASSISTANT STATE'S ATTORNEY: Yes, of course. The document is marked as Exhibit 1 and is being handed to the Grand Jurors.

ASSISTANT STATE'S ATTORNEY: Are there any other questions?

[No audible response.]

ASSISTANT STATE'S ATTORNEY: Okay. Ladies and gentlemen, the applicable law has been read to you and you have a copy of the statute for reference. I will now leave the room so that you may discuss the evidence presented and determine whether or not to issue a true bill.

CIRCUIT COURT OF THE STATE OF ILLINOIS
FOR THE COUNTY OF COLUMBIA

The People of the State of Illinois,		)	
	Plaintiff,	)	CASE NO. GJ140212A
v.		)	
		)	INDICTMENT
Rex Berry		)	
	Defendant.	)	

COUNT I

The Grand Jurors chosen, selected, and sworn, in and for the County of Columbia, in the State of Illinois, in the name and by the authority of the People of the State of Illinois, upon their oaths, present that on or about July 2, 2014, at and within the County of Columbia, REX BERRY committed the offense of: POSSESSION OF A CONTROLLED SUBSTANCE, HEROIN, in that he did knowingly and unlawfully have in his possession less than 15 grams of a substance containing a controlled substance, heroin, in violation of Chapter 720, Act 570, Section 401(c)(1) of the Illinois Compiled Statutes.

A TRUE BILL

Suzanne George
Foreperson of the Grand Jury

Presented by the Foreperson of the Grand Jury in the presence of the Grand Jury, in open Circuit Court of the State of Illinois, within and for the County of Columbia, and filed as a record in said Court this 3rd day of July, 2014.

CIRCUIT COURT OF THE STATE OF ILLINOIS
FOR THE COUNTY OF COLUMBIA

The People of the State of Illinois, Plaintiff, v. Rex Berry, DOB 01/12/88 Defendant.	))))))	WARRANT OF ARREST

THE STATE OF ILLINOIS: To any Peace Officer in the State of Illinois, Greetings:

An Information or Indictment, having been filed in open court before me, and it appears from the Information or Indictment, or Affidavit filed with such document, that there is probable cause to believe that the public offense of:

> POSSESSION OF A CONTROLLED SUBSTANCE,
> HEROIN, a felony, has been committed, and that
> Rex Berry committed that crime.

YOU ARE THEREFORE COMMANDED to arrest the above-named defendant forthwith and bring the defendant before this Court, or before the nearest or most accessible magistrate, for setting bail. If the defendant has fled justice, you shall pursue the defendant into any other county of this state and there arrest the defendant. The Court finds reasonable grounds to believe defendant will not appear upon a summons.

Bail is set in the amount of $10,000.00.

Dated this 3rd day of July 2014.

This Warrant may be served day or night.

____
JUDGE

Served: Date: ________________________ By: ________________________

GRAND JURY EXERCISE

NAME ______________________________

COURSE ______________________________

DATE ______________________________

Please provide full and complete responses to the following five questions:

1. When and where did the grand jury system begin? What is the purpose of a grand jury today? Do all states use the grand jury procedure?

2. How does an Indictment differ from a Complaint and Information? What is a "true bill"?

3. How does the role of a grand juror differ from that of a trial juror?

4. Generally, how many grand jurors will hear evidence presented? Generally, how many jurors serve on a jury trial?

5. Grand jury proceedings are held in secret without the presence of a judge, defendant, or defense counsel. Can this system possibly be fair? Explain your response.

PART II

PRE-TRIAL MOTIONS

KEY TERMS		
affidavit	good-faith exception	motion to suppress
arrest	illegally seized evidence	plain view
confession	interrogation	reasonable suspicion
consent search	landmark case	self-incrimination
exclusionary rule	*Miranda* triggers	search warrant
frisk	*Miranda* warning	*Terry* stop

INTRODUCTION

People v. Potter

Penny Potter hears a knock at her front door. She opens it to find a Columbia City police officer. The officer is looking for her friend, Nick. Penny tells the officer Nick isn't there. The officer wants to see for himself. Penny lets the officer in to do just that. The next thing Penny knows, she's being handcuffed and arrested for possession of cocaine. Penny has entered a plea of not guilty and her public defender has filed a motion to suppress the evidence. You may decide for yourself whether the cocaine will be admitted at Penny's trial.

People v. Freeburg

Freddie Freeburg is sitting in his living room watching television. He thinks he hears someone enter his house through the back door. The next thing Freddie knows, a Columbia City police officer is standing in his living room with a gun pointed at him. The officer picks up from the coffee table Freddie's bag of weed, a scale and his bong, and leaves without saying a word to him. A week later, Freddie is picked up on a warrant and finds out he has been charged with possession with intent to deliver marijuana and possession of paraphernalia. Freddie has entered pleas of not guilty. His public defender has filed a motion to suppress the evidence. You may decide for yourself whether the evidence will be admitted at Freddie's trial.

People v. Martin

Rob Martin is standing alone on a street corner. The next thing he knows, a Columbia City police officer has approached him and is frisking him. The officer seizes Rob's gun from the waistband of his jeans. Rob is placed under arrest and transported to the station for questioning. Rob has been charged with the felony offense of defacing identification marks of firearms. Rob's public defender has filed a motion to suppress evidence in his case. You may decide for yourself what the ruling will be.

CONSTITUTIONAL RIGHTS

It is common in our criminal justice system for defendants to allege a violation of their Constitutional rights under the Fourth, Fifth, and Sixth Amendments. It is crucial for law enforcement officers, criminal lawyers, and judges anywhere to have a thorough understanding of their State and Federal constitutions and be aware of the latest court rulings. Columbia County is no exception, as you will see.

STOP AND FRISK

Fourth Amendment law is one of the most dynamic and changing areas of the law. Since the 1968 landmark decision of the U.S. Supreme Court in *Terry v. Ohio,* 393 U.S. 1, officers routinely engage with individuals in brief encounters referred to as a "stop and frisk," based upon reasonable suspicion. Officers must have a reasonable belief that criminal activity has occurred, is occurring, or is about to occur to detain the person. Officers may conduct an open-handed frisk of the outer clothing if it is reasonable to believe the person may be armed and pose a safety risk to the officer. Keep in mind that the "frisk" is not automatic with the "stop."

In the absence of reasonable suspicion for the stop, or for the frisk, any contraband seized from the individual may not be used as evidence against the person. The remedy exists in the exclusionary rule for a defendant who believes an officer has seized evidence from them unlawfully. A criminal defendant may file a pre-trial motion asking the court to suppress the evidence; in other words, exclude its admission at trial. If the evidence is excluded from admission at trial, the case is not automatically dismissed. But, the prosecutor must decide whether the necessary elements at trial can be established without the evidence. If, for example, a defendant is charged with possession of cocaine and the court grants the defendant's motion to suppress the cocaine from evidence, the prosecutor is not going to be able to prove the case and must dismiss the charge.

SEARCH WARRANTS

The Fourth Amendment provides protection from unreasonable searches and seizures conducted by the government either with or without a warrant. In order to obtain a search warrant, an officer must establish under oath for a judge that probable cause exists to believe that identifiable evidence of a crime exists at a particular location. In executing the search warrant, officers may search in areas only where the items listed in the warrant may be found.

EXCLUSIONARY RULE—GOOD FAITH EXCEPTION

The exclusionary rule was created by the U.S. Supreme Court to deter police from violating Fourth Amendment principles. (Why seize evidence from an individual unlawfully if it cannot be used against them at trial?) Illinois provides a "good faith" exception to the exclusionary rule. A prosecutor may argue to the court that the officer's conduct in obtaining the evidence was done with a reasonable and objective good faith belief that the conduct was proper, and therefore, the evidence should not be suppressed. Generally, if the police made what appears to be an honest mistake, the exclusionary rule should not apply.

CONSENT SEARCH

There is a general preference for governmental searches to be conducted with a warrant, but many exceptions to the warrant requirement exist. A common exception is the consent search. An officer without a warrant, even without probable cause, may ask an individual for consent to search. While many restrictions exist, for our purposes, keep in mind that the person granting consent to a search must do so voluntarily. The person granting consent to search may limit the search (for example, saying, "you may search the passenger compartment of my car but not the trunk") and may revoke consent at any time.

PLAIN VIEW

Just as officers conducting a lawful frisk may rely upon the concept of plain feel and seize an item readily recognizable as contraband, an officer may rely upon the doctrine of plain view. If an officer, while in a lawful position, sees contraband in the open, it may be seized as evidence without a warrant and used at a subsequent trial.

MIRANDA

The Fifth Amendment affords criminal defendants many rights, including the right against self-incrimination. With the 1966 landmark decision of the U.S. Supreme Court in *Miranda v. Arizona,* 384 U.S. 436, "Miranda" has become part of our everyday language. Not everyone understands, however, that the *Miranda* warning need not automatically be given to the suspect at the time of arrest. There are two triggers for *Miranda*: 1) custody, and 2) interrogation. If a person is arrested but not interrogated, then the warning is not required. Generally, a person is deemed "in custody" when that person reasonably believes he or she is no longer free to go.

A suspect who is in custody and is about to be interrogated by police has the right to waive, or give up, their right against self-incrimination. The burden is on the government to show that the defendant voluntarily and knowingly waived their right. To meet this burden, officers often begin an interrogation at the police station by having the suspect sign a standardized waiver form.

MOTION TO SUPPRESS

The exclusionary rule applies to a confession as well as to tangible evidence. For a defendant who feels his confession was obtained in violation of the Fifth Amendment, the remedy is the same—file a motion to suppress with the court and seek a hearing. While the prosecution always has the burden at trial of proving a criminal defendant guilty beyond a reasonable doubt, the burden is on the defendant at a suppression hearing.

Statute
MOTION TO SUPPRESS
725 ILCS 5/114-12 MOTION TO SUPPRESS EVIDENCE ILLEGALLY SEIZED

(a) A defendant aggrieved by an unlawful search and seizure may move the court for the return of property and to suppress as evidence anything so obtained on the ground that:

1. The search and seizure without a warrant was illegal; or
2. The search and seizure with a warrant was illegal because the warrant is insufficient on its face; the evidence seized is not that described in the warrant; there was not probable cause for the issuance of the warrant; or, the warrant was illegally executed.

(b) The motion shall be in writing and state facts showing wherein the search and seizure were unlawful. The judge shall receive evidence on any issue of fact necessary to determine the motion, and the burden of proving that the search and seizure were unlawful shall be on the defendant. If the motion is granted the property shall be restored, unless otherwise subject to lawful detention, and it shall not be admissible in evidence against the movant at any trial.

1. If a defendant seeks to suppress evidence because of the conduct of a peace officer in obtaining the evidence, the State may urge that the peace officer's conduct was taken in a reasonable and objective good faith belief that the conduct was proper and that the evidence discovered should not be suppressed if otherwise admissible. The court shall not suppress evidence which is otherwise admissible in a criminal proceeding if the court determines that the evidence was seized by a peace officer who acted in good faith.
2. "Good faith" means whenever a peace officer obtains evidence:
   (i) pursuant to a search or an arrest warrant obtained from a neutral and detached judge, which warrant is free from obvious defects other than non-deliberate errors in preparation, and contains no material misrepresentation by any agent of the State, and the officer reasonably believed the warrant to be valid; or
   (ii) pursuant to a warrantless search incident to an arrest for violation of a statute or local ordinance which is later declared unconstitutional or otherwise invalidated.

(c) The motion shall be made before trial unless opportunity therefor did not exist or the defendant was not aware of the grounds for the motion.

The defendant has been charged with Possession of a controlled substance—Cocaine. Defendant has filed a pre-trial Motion to Suppress Evidence. The defendant seeks to have the cocaine seized by the officer excluded from her trial. The following is a transcript from the hearing on the defendant's motion.

ONCE COURT CONVENED, THE FOLLOWING EVIDENCE WAS PRESENTED:

PRESENT: JUDGE
CLERK
BAILIFF
ASSISTANT STATE'S ATTORNEY
PUBLIC DEFENDER
DEFENDANT
WITNESS – OFFICER

THE COURT: Would the clerk please call the next case for hearing?

CLERK: *People v. Potter,* defendant appears with counsel for a hearing on her Motion to Suppress Evidence.

THE COURT: The defendant's trial is scheduled to begin one month from today's date. The defendant has filed a written motion alleging the cocaine at issue was seized by law enforcement in violation of the defendant's constitutional rights. The court will now hear evidence on any issue of fact necessary to determine the motion. The burden of proving that the search and seizure were unlawful is on the defendant. Counsel you may call your witness.

PUBLIC DEFENDER: I call Officer Friendly to the stand.

[The officer is sworn and takes the witness stand.]

TESTIMONY OF DEFENSE WITNESS—DIRECT EXAMINATION

BY: PUBLIC DEFENDER

Q: Please state your name and occupation for the record.

A: Officer Friendly, I am employed with the Columbia City Police Department.

Q: I would like to draw your attention to the day you went to my client's residence. Do you recall your actions once you arrived at her apartment?

A: Yes, vividly.

Q: Please tell the court why you went to my client's home that day.

A: I went to the residence as part of an investigation I was working on. I wanted to speak with an individual who I understood sometimes stayed at the residence.

Q: What happened once you got to my client's residence?

A: I knocked on the door. The defendant answered. I identified myself as an officer and asked if Nick Mann was there. She replied no. I asked the defendant if she minded if I looked around.

Q: How did my client respond?

A: She said, "Come on in, you can see for yourself that he is not here."

Q: What did you do then?

A: I walked through the door into the living room area. I walked through the kitchen and then down the hallway to the master bedroom. Once inside the bedroom, I checked under the bed and opened the closet door.

Q: What did you do next?

A: I noticed an armoire, or wardrobe sort of chest, in the room. Both doors to the chest opened from the middle. Once I opened the doors, I observed a mirror with a white powdery substance on it along with a razor blade.

Q: What did you do then?

A: I seized the substance and conducted a field test that provided a positive reaction to cocaine. I then placed the defendant under arrest.

Q: Did you discontinue your search for Mr. Mann once you seized the white powdery substance?

A: Yes, it became apparent that the subject I was looking for was not within the residence.

Q: Officer, at the time you went to my client's residence, did you have a physical description for Mr. Mann?

A: I did.

Q: What is the height and weight of the individual you were looking for?

A: As I recall, Mann is about 5'11" and probably weighs 185.

Q: Officer, what was the size of this wardrobe, or chest, that you have referred to today?

A: Oh, it's hard to say but I would guess it was about four feet high, and about four feet long, and probably three feet deep.

PUBLIC DEFENDER: Your Honor, at this time I would like to have something brought into the courtroom and marked as an exhibit.

THE COURT: Go ahead.

PUBLIC DEFENDER: Bailiff, if you could please assist my associate who is in the hallway. Thanks.

BAILIFF: Where do you want this?

PUBLIC DEFENDER: If you could please set it right here in the well of the courtroom. Your Honor, is that okay?

THE COURT: For the time being. Let's have this marked as Defense exhibit A for identification. Counsel, do you want to identify this?

PUBLIC DEFENDER: Yes, Your Honor. Officer, looking at what has been marked as Defense exhibit A for identification, do you recognize this?

A: Why, yes. That is the wardrobe, or chest, in which I located the cocaine.

Q: How can you tell for sure it is the same piece of furniture?

A: It is unique because the numerals 420 are hand-carved into the right side of the chest.

Q: Does the chest appear to be in substantially the same condition today as when you saw it in my client's residence?

A: Yes.

PUBLIC DEFENDER: At this time, I move to admit Defense exhibit A.

THE COURT: Any objection?

ASSISTANT STATE'S ATTORNEY: Ah, no Your Honor.

PUBLIC DEFENDER: With the court's permission, I would like to ask the officer to momentarily step down from the stand and approach the chest.

THE COURT: Very well. Officer, if you would, please?

Q: Officer, if you would please use this tape measure, I would like you to give us the dimensions of this chest.

A: Very well. Let's see, it's 36 inches so that would be three feet high. Ah, it is 30 inches long so that would be two and a half feet long. And it is 20 inches deep.

PUBLIC DEFENDER: Thank you, Officer. You may return to the witness stand. I don't have any additional questions for the witness.

THE COURT: Does the prosecutor have any questions?

ASSISTANT STATE'S ATTORNEY: Just a couple.

CROSS EXAMINATION OF WITNESS

BY: ASSISTANT STATE'S ATTORNEY

Q: Officer, just to clarify your earlier testimony, the doors of this chest were both closed when you entered the bedroom, is that correct?

A: Correct.

Q: With the doors closed, you couldn't tell whether there were shelves or anything built into the interior of the chest, could you?

A: No, I could not.

ASSISTANT STATE'S ATTORNEY: Thank you. Nothing further.

THE COURT: Does the defense have questions on redirect?

PUBLIC DEFENDER: No.

THE COURT: Very well. Officer you may step down.

THE COURT: Does the defense have additional witnesses?

PUBLIC DEFENDER: No, Your Honor.

THE COURT: At this time, I will hear arguments of counsel and will then give you my ruling.

CONSENT SEARCH EXERCISE

NAME ____

COURSE ____

DATE ____

Please provide full and complete responses to the following five questions:

1. As the public defender, what argument would you make to the judge that the cocaine should be excluded from admission at trial? Be persuasive.

2. As the prosecutor, what argument would you make to the judge that the cocaine was seized lawfully by the officer and therefore should be admitted into evidence at the subsequent trial?

3. After considering the arguments presented by counsel, if you were the judge in this case, would you grant or deny the defendant's motion to suppress the evidence? Why?

4. If the defendant's motion is granted, what is likely to happen with the pending charge of Possession of a Controlled Substance—Cocaine?

5. At the time the officer went to the defendant's residence, what things could the officer have done so that the defendant would not feel her Fourth Amendment rights had been violated?

The defendant has been charged with Possession with intent to deliver marijuana and Possession of drug paraphernalia. Defendant has filed a pre-trial Motion to Suppress Evidence. The defendant seeks to have the marijuana and paraphernalia seized by the officer excluded from his trial. The following is a transcript from the hearing on the defendant's motion.

ONCE COURT CONVENED, THE FOLLOWING EVIDENCE WAS PRESENTED:

PRESENT: JUDGE
CLERK
BAILIFF
ASSISTANT STATE'S ATTORNEY
PUBLIC DEFENDER
DEFENDANT
WITNESS – OFFICER

THE COURT: Okay, we are on the record in *People v. Freeburg*. The defendant appears with counsel for a hearing on a Motion to Suppress Evidence prior to the upcoming trial. Let's see. The defendant's motion alleges that marijuana and drug paraphernalia were seized by the officer in violation of the defendant's Fourth Amendment right against unlawful search and seizure. The court will now hear evidence on any issue of fact necessary to determine the motion. The burden at this hearing is upon the defense. Counsel you may call your witness.

PUBLIC DEFENDER: I call Officer Walker.

[The officer affirms and takes the witness stand.]

TESTIMONY OF DEFENSE WITNESS—DIRECT EXAMINATION

BY: PUBLIC DEFENDER

Q: Please state your name for the record, and tell us where you are employed.

A: My name is Pat Walker and I am a patrol officer with the Columbia City Police Department in Columbia City, Illinois.

Q: Officer Walker, I would like to draw your attention to exactly two months prior to today. Did you assist other officers in executing a search warrant on that day?

A: Yes I did.

Q: Were you involved in the preparation of the Affidavit for Search Warrant or preparation of the Search Warrant itself?

A: No. The drug task force was involved in preparing the warrant and getting it signed by a judge. I was asked by my supervisor to assist in the execution of the warrant.

Q: What did you do?

A: I had just completed my shift on patrol. I was asked to stay overtime to help the drug task force and the detectives execute the warrant. I sat in on the briefing at the department as everybody was assigned different duties. I was assigned to go to the back door of the residence, and once officers entered from the front, I would then enter from the back.

Q: According to the search warrant signed by the Judge, what was the address of the place to be searched?

A: It was 1776 Asbury Court, apartment 2B, Columbia City, Illinois.

Q: What type of building was this?

A: Well, it was sort of a four-plex. There were four buildings there on Asbury Court, each with four residences, so in building number 2, the residences were identified as A, B, C, and D at both the front and back doors. Each residence had a ground floor entry.

Q: Okay, I think I understand. So, what did you do once you arrived at 1776 Asbury Court?

A: I went around back as I was supposed to and waited to hear on my radio that officers had secured the residence from the front so that I could enter.

Q: What happened then?

A: Once I got the all clear on my radio, I entered the apartment.

Q: But there was a problem, wasn't there?

A: Well, yeah, but I didn't know it at the time.

Q: Go on, what happened?

A: Well, I went through the back door, I had my service revolver drawn, and I proceeded through the back of the residence towards the living room, where I could see there was a light on.

Q: What happened once you got to the living room?

A: I observed the defendant sitting on the couch. In front of him was a coffee table. On the coffee table, I observed a scale along with a baggie containing what appeared to be a green leafy substance. On an end table to the right of the defendant was a huge bong, or water pipe.

Q: What happened next?

A: Well, I was standing there with my weapon drawn, and I was looking for my fellow officers. But, they weren't there. I got on my radio and asked the Sergeant where he was.

Q: What was the reply?

A: He told me they were in the apartment, and he asked where I was. I told him I was in the apartment. He asked me which apartment I was in. I told him I was in 2D. That's when he told me I was supposed to be in 2B.

Q: What did you do then?

A: I grabbed the scale, the bong and the baggie, and I left out the same door I had come in.

Q: Did you say anything to my client?

A: No.

Q: Did my client say anything to you?

A: No. He just sat and watched me the whole time. He looked pretty dazed and confused.

Q: What did you do once you left my client's apartment?

A: Well, I secured the evidence in my patrol car and then I went to assist the officers who were conducting the search in apartment 2B. Once that was completed, that I took the items from 2D to the Evidence Technician for safekeeping. The substance in the baggie tested positive for marijuana, so I looked up who lives in 2D. I then sought charges.

PUBLIC DEFENDER: Thank you. Nothing further.

THE COURT: Cross-examination, counsel?

ASSISTANT STATE'S ATTORNEY: Thank you, Your Honor.

CROSS EXAMINATION OF WITNESS

BY: ASSISTANT STATE'S ATTORNEY

Q: Officer, did you ever look at the address listed on the search warrant?

A: No. At the briefing, I just listened to what apartment we were to enter.

Q: Why is it then, that you entered 2D instead of 2B?

A: Well, I don't know. I guess I just heard wrong. I suppose I was tired.

Q: Why did you seize the items?

A: Because it was contraband and it was in plain view.

ASSISTANT STATE'S ATTORNEY: Thank you, officer. I have no other questions.

THE COURT: Any cross-examination counsel?

PUBLIC DEFENDER: No, nothing further.

THE COURT: Do you wish to call any other witnesses?

PUBLIC DEFENDER: No, that's all I have Your Honor.

THE COURT: Do the People intend to call any witnesses?

ASSISTANT STATE'S ATTORNEY: No.

THE COURT: Very well. At this time, I will listen to argument of counsel and then issue my decision on the motion.

"GOOD FAITH" EXERCISE

NAME ______________________________

COURSE ______________________________

DATE ______________________________

Please provide full and complete responses to the following five questions:

1. As the public defender, what argument would you make to the judge that the marijuana along with the scale and bong should be excluded from admission at trial? Be persuasive.

2. As the prosecutor, what argument would you make to the judge that the items seized by the officer should be admitted into evidence at the upcoming trial?

3. After considering the arguments presented by counsel, if you were the judge in this case, would you grant or deny the defendant's motion to suppress the evidence? Why?

4. If the judge grants the defendant's motion, will the evidence be returned to the defendant? Explain.

5. Consider the following scenario. The officers intended to obtain a search warrant for apartment 2B. Officers entered and searched apartment 2B, seizing the evidence listed on the search warrant. However, the individual who prepared the warrant typed "2D" for the address instead of "2B." Should the evidence be excluded? State your reasoning.

Statutes

CONFESSION

725 ILCS 5/114-10 MOTION TO PRODUCE CONFESSION

(a) On motion of a defendant in any criminal case made prior to trial the court shall order the State to furnish the defendant with a copy of any written confession made to any law enforcement officer of this State or any other State and a list of the witnesses to its making and acknowledgment. If the defendant has made an oral confession a list of the witnesses to its making shall be furnished.

(b) The list of witnesses may upon notice and motion be amended by the Sate prior to trial.

(c) No such confession shall be received in evidence which has not been furnished in compliance with subsection (a) of this Section unless the court is satisfied that the prosecutor was unaware of the existence of such confession prior to trial and that he could not have become aware of such in the exercise of due diligence.

725 ILCS 5/114-11 MOTION TO SUPPRESS CONFESSION

(a) Prior to the trial of any criminal case a defendant may move to suppress as evidence any confession given by him on the ground that it was not voluntary.

CIRCUIT COURT OF THE STATE OF ILLINOIS
FOR THE COUNTY OF COLUMBIA

The People of the State of Illinois,	)	
Plaintiff,	)	Case No. CF14-0951
v.	)	
	)	MOTION TO SUPPRESS
Robert E. Martin, DOB 3/15/96	)	
Defendant.	)	

The defendant, Robert E. Martin, by and through the Columbia County Public Defender's Office, pursuant to 725 ILCS 5/114-11 and 725 ILCS 5/114-12, moves this court to suppress any and all statements made by him to law enforcement officials of the Columbia City Police Department in relation to the above-referenced case, and further to suppress evidence, to wit: a Glock 19 Pistol, 9mm, seized by law enforcement in relation to the above-referenced case.

In support of this motion the defendant relies upon the memorandum and transcript attached hereto.

Respectfully submitted,

Chris Kelley

Robert E. Martin
By Chris Kelley, Counsel for defendant

CIRCUIT COURT OF THE STATE OF ILLINOIS
FOR THE COUNTY OF COLUMBIA

The People of the State of Illinois, Plaintiff,	)	Case No. CF14-0951
v.	)))	
Robert E. Martin, DOB 3/15/96 Defendant.	))	

MEMORANDUM IN SUPPORT OF
DEFENDANT'S MOTION TO SUPPRESS CONFESSION AND EVIDENCE

The defendant, Robert E. Martin, by and through the Columbia County Public Defender's Office, pursuant to 725 ILCS 5/114-11 and 725 ILCS 5/114-12 moves this court to suppress any and all statements made by him to law enforcement officials of the Columbia City Police Department in relation to the above-referenced case, and further to suppress evidence, to wit: a Glock 19 Pistol, 9 mm, seized by law enforcement in relation to the above-referenced case. The defendant submits the following in support of this motion:

1. The defendant, Robert E. Martin, DOB 3/15/96, was lawfully at the intersection of 10th and Mayfield Streets, Columbia City, Illinois at approximately 1:10 A.M.
2. The defendant was approached by Jack Friendly who is an officer employed by the Columbia City Police Department.
3. The defendant was wearing blue jeans and an oversized black T-shirt.
4. Officer Friendly immediately conducted a pat-down, or frisk, of the defendant. The officer retrieved from the defendant's waistband a Glock, matte finish, 9mm semi-automatic pistol with a 4.02" barrel. No serial number.
5. The defendant was then searched, placed into a patrol car, and transported to the Columbia City Police Department.
6. The defendant was taken to an interrogation room and was interrogated by Officer Friendly without first being made aware of his rights.
7. The defendant's rights were violated during the course of the interrogation. The defendant was not advised of his *Miranda* rights under the Fifth Amendment and, even if he had been advised, the defendant was in no state to knowingly or intelligently waive those rights. The defendant's specific request to consult with an attorney was denied by the officer.
8. The defendant was then booked into the Columbia County Jail on the charge of Aggravated Possession of a Stolen Firearm.

9. The defendant is being investigated on charges of Attempted Murder, Delivery of a Controlled Substance, Heroin, and Theft.
10. The defendant did not have an opportunity to speak with a lawyer until the judge at his initial appearance appointed the Public Defender's Office to represent him.

The defendant contends that his Fourth Amendment right against unlawful search and seizure was violated, as well as his rights under the Fifth and Fourteenth Amendments to counsel and due process. The defendant asks this court to suppress the gun and any statements made to law enforcement officials in relation to this case.

Respectfully submitted,

Chris Kelley

Robert E. Martin
By Chris Kelley, Counsel for defendant

The suspect is in custody and has been brought to the Columbia City Police Department and placed in an interrogation room. Officer Jack Friendly interrogates the suspect. The interrogation was recorded. The following is a transcript from the interrogation.

INTERVIEW OF ROBERT E. MARTIN CONDUCTED BY OFFICER JACK FRIENDLY:

JF: Come on in and have a seat in that chair by the table over there. I'll just pull up this chair here by the door. Okay, let's see, it is now 01:35 Sunday morning. I'm Jack Friendly and I want to take a minute to chat with you. Your full name is Robert E. Martin, is that right?

REM: Yeah.

JF: What do you go by? Bob? Bobby?

REM: What? Oh, Rob.

JF: Are you feeling okay? You don't look so hot.

REM: Man, I am [inaudible] trashed.

JF: Well then, I'll try to get through this as quickly as possible. What were you doing on the corner of Mayfield at that time of the morning, looking to score?

REM: I need to use the john.

JF: Come on, let's get through this. Am I going to find track marks on you, or are you chasing the dragon?

REM: You got anything to eat in here?

JF: Hey Rob, focus on me for a second. Where did you get that gun? The Glock.

REM: I don't know what you're talking about.

JF: I'm talking about the 9mm I took off you this morning when I stopped you at the corner at Mayfield and 10th Streets. Can you remember back that far?

REM: Man, I was just out on the street, taking care of business. I don't know why you have to hassle me. I wasn't doing nothing.

JF: Well, 10th and Mayfield is a high crime area in Columbia City. But then, I guess you would know that.

REM: Can I smoke in here?

JF: No. There's no serial number on that gun. Where'd you get it?

REM: Man, I've got to piss like a racehorse.

JF: Sit down. You're not going anywhere until you tell me something.

REM: What do you want from me, man?

JF: I want to know what you've been up to, and I want to know where you got the gun. So, just sit your ass down.

REM: Should I have a lawyer or something?

JF: Hey, if you haven't done anything, then what do you need a lawyer for?

REM: Look, yeah. I got a problem. I got everybody in the world out after me. You can't live out there without a gun. Yeah, I stole that thing like two weeks ago. I was car hopping and found it under a seat. I worked my ass off to get that serial number scratched off. That thing's mine.

JF: Who's after you?

REM: Dude named Jacko.

JF: What's his full name?

REM: Man, I don't know. Jacko is all I know. He's been fronting me decks, and I've been selling them.

JF: Heroin?

REM: I had this cash; money I had to pay back Jacko with, but I got ripped off. So then I started tapping the bags thinking I could make some extra cash. But now I got some guys after me saying I shorted them.

JF: Now that's a shame. Put that cigarette down.

REM: Tonight I was walking down 10th Street looking for somebody I know. I need a place to crash and get my head together. Only Jacko spotted me. He was demanding his cash, which I don't have. He shoved me down an alley and slammed me up against the building. He was right in my face demanding his money. I pulled the Glock out of my waistband and fired. He swore at me and took off running. I think I hit him but he took off okay.

JF: Who do you use as a fence?

REM: What? Oh. Usually when I'm digging in cars I'm looking for cash, but if I find some electronics or maybe a leather coat or something, I take it to Joe's Pawnshop on 12th. He doesn't give me much, but at least it's something.

JF: Here, I want you to sign this form for me. It's a rights waiver form. You know, *Miranda?*

REM: What? Man, I can't even read that thing.

JF: You don't have to. I can read it to you. First, it says you don't have to answer any questions or say anything. Second, anything you say or do can be used as evidence against you in a criminal trial. Third, you have the right to talk privately to a lawyer before, during, or after questioning. If you can't afford a lawyer, one will be arranged for you at no expense. Okay? See, here, I'm going to sign it. Now you sign it.

REM: Where? Fine. I've told you everything. Now can I go?

JF: Oh no. Now you have to tell me everything you've told me. Again.

REM: That ain't gonna happen.

JF: Sit down. Where are you going? Hey. Are you actually peeing in the corner? Shut the tape off. [End of recording.]

CIRCUIT COURT OF THE STATE OF ILLINOIS
FOR THE COUNTY OF COLUMBIA

The People of the State of Illinois, Plaintiff,	))	Case No. CF14-0951
v.	))	
Robert E. Martin, DOB 3/15/96 Defendant.	))	

MEMORANDUM IN OPPOSITION TO DEFENDANT'S
MOTION TO SUPPRESS CONFESSION AND EVIDENCE

The State's Attorney's Office by and through Mary M. Fitzsimmons, State's Attorney for Columbia County, responds in opposition to defendant's motion as follows:

1. The area of 10th and Mayfield Streets in Columbia City is well known to police officers as being a high-crime area. Officer Friendly was assigned to patrol the area as part of an organized effort to decrease drug, prostitution, and violent crimes in that area.
2. Officer Friendly had reasonable suspicion to approach the defendant and to conduct a brief investigatory stop.
3. In accordance with an investigatory, or *Terry* stop, the officer was justified in conducting a pat down for weapons. Given that defendant was in what is known to be a high-crime area, in the early morning hours, it was reasonable for the officer to suspect the defendant was armed and dangerous.
4. Officer Friendly was justified in retrieving the weapon from the defendant during the course of the contact. Since the defendant was not lawfully in possession of the weapon, and since the weapon did not have a serial number, the officer lawfully seized the gun and arrested the defendant for possession.
5. Although contested, Officer Friendly contends he advised the defendant of his *Miranda* rights while transporting the defendant to the police department. Although there is no recording of any conversation during transport, the defendant subsequently signed a rights waiver form during his interview at the station. A defendant can knowingly and intentionally waive his right to remain silent and his right to counsel during questioning.
6. The defendant was not denied counsel in violation of his Fifth Amendment rights during his interview. A defendant must articulate a desire for counsel. That did not occur in the instant case.

7. The defendant is an adult and is presumed to be of sound mind and of normal intelligence. A defendant can knowingly and voluntarily waive his right to remain silent and his right to counsel during questioning.

The People contend the defendant's constitutional rights were not violated in any way and ask this court to deny the defendant's motion to suppress and allow the defendant's statements and the gun to be admitted into evidence at trial.

Respectfully submitted,

Mary M. Fitzsimmons

Mary M. Fitzsimmons
State's Attorney for Columbia County

Statute
MOTION TO SUPPRESS CONFESSION/EVIDENCE
720 ILCS 5/24-5 DEFACING IDENTIFICATION MARKS OF FIREARMS

(a) Any person who shall knowingly or intentionally change, alter, remove or obliterate the name of the importer's or manufacturer's serial number of any firearm commits a Class 2 felony.

(b) A person who possesses any firearm upon which any such importer's or manufacturer's serial number has been changed, altered, removed or obliterated commits a Class 3 felony.

(c) Nothing in this Section shall prevent a person from making repairs, replacement of parts, or other changes to a firearm if those repairs, replacement of parts, or changes cause the removal of the name of the maker, model, or other marks of identification other than the serial number on the firearm's frame or receiver.

(d) A prosecution for a violation of this Section may be commenced within 6 years after the commission of the offense.

SUPPRESSION OF CONFESSION AND EVIDENCE EXERCISE

NAME ____

COURSE ____

DATE ____

Please provide full and complete responses to the following questions:

1. According to the U.S. Supreme Court's decision in the landmark case, *Terry v. Ohio,* what is required in order for an officer to briefly detain an individual? Under what circumstances may the officer conduct a frisk of that individual? Is it automatic?

2. According to the U.S. Supreme Court's decision in the landmark case, *Miranda v. Arizona*, is an officer required to advise the arrestee of his or her rights immediately upon arrest? Explain under what circumstances an officer must provide *Miranda* rights to a suspect.

3. After reviewing the documents provided in the case of *People v. Robert E. Martin*, was the officer justified in stopping the defendant? Was the frisk justified? List factors to support your answer.

4. If the judge were to rule the stop was unreasonable, was the arrest lawful? If the judge were to rule the arrest was unlawful, could the gun be used against the defendant at trial? From reading the statute, does it appear the defendant was in violation of that law? Explain.

5. If you were the judge in this case, how would you rule on the defendant's motion to suppress:

a. statements made at the police station?
b. the gun?

Explain your reasoning.

PART III

TRIALS: PETTY AND MISDEMEANOR OFFENSES

KEY TERMS		
acquit	direct examination	objection
affirmation	due process	presumption of innocence
beyond reasonable doubt	elements	rebuttal
chain of custody	exhibit	rules of evidence
contempt of court	hearsay	*stare decisis*
court trial	impound-inventory	venue
cross-examination	judicial notice	void for vagueness
delinquent	oath	warrant

INTRODUCTION

Part III contains transcripts from three different trials. Misdemeanor crimes are less serious than felony offenses. In Illinois misdemeanors are classified for the purpose of sentencing as either Class A, Class B or Class C. "Misdemeanor" is defined in 730 ILCS 5/5-1-14 as any offense for which a sentence to a term of imprisonment in other than a penitentiary for less than one year may be imposed. Illinois also has petty, or business, offenses, to which a sentence of a fine only is provided.

For each of the trials that follow, you will have the opportunity to don the judge's robe, apply the facts to the law, pick up the gavel and decide for yourself whether the accused is guilty or not guilty. Good luck.

UNLAWFUL USE OF WEAPON TRIAL

Officer McGillicuddy stopped a vehicle for having an air freshener hanging from the rear view mirror. Once the driver opened the glove compartment to retrieve the requested documents, McGillicuddy observed a handgun inside. The driver had not been issued a Firearm Owners Identification card (FOID) in the State of Illinois. Was it a lawful traffic stop? Is it a slam dunk case for the prosecution? Be sure to read the laws carefully!

ILLEGAL POSSESSION OF ALCOHOL TRIAL

Do you know a beer when you see one? Or smell one? Officer Pat Walker with the Columbia City Police Department cited a passenger for possessing open alcohol in a vehicle. What are the elements of this offense? What evidence must the prosecutor establish in order for the defendant to be found guilty? May an officer rely upon their senses? Will we require forensics in all cases? Even a petty offense? You be the judge.

DISORDERLY CONDUCT TRIAL

This proceeding differs from the previous trials in two respects: the accused is eleven years old, and the defense is challenging the constitutionality of the law under which the juvenile has been charged. The juvenile justice system is separate and distinct from adult court. Illinois law defines "delinquent minor" as any minor who prior to his or her 18th birthday has violated or attempted to violate . . . any Federal or State law, county or municipal ordinance classified as a misdemeanor." Juveniles possess many of the same rights as adults. The public defender representing Garth Ames does not dispute the conduct his client is alleged to have engaged in, but rather, challenges the statute itself. Ask yourself: do you understand what conduct is prohibited by this law?

Statute
UNLAWFUL USE OF WEAPON AND FOID VIOLATION
720 ILCS 5/24-1 UNLAWFUL USE OF WEAPONS

Sec. 24-1

(a) A person commits the offense of unlawful use of weapons when he knowingly:

• • • • • • • • • • • • • • • • • • • •

4. Carries or possesses in any vehicle or concealed on or about his person except when on his land or in his own abode, legal dwelling, or fixed place of business, or on the land or in the legal dwelling of another person as an invitee with that person's permission any pistol, revolver, stun gun, or taser or other firearm, except that this subsection (a) (4) does not apply to or affect transportation of weapons that meet one of the following conditions:
   - (i) are broken down in a non-functioning state; or
   - (ii) are not immediately accessible; or
   - (iii) are unloaded and enclosed in a case, firearm carrying box, shipping box or other container by a person who has been issued a currently valid Firearm Owner's Identification Card; or

• • • • • • • • • • • • • • • • • • • •

430 ILCS 65/2 FIREARM OWNER'S IDENTIFICATION CARD REQUIRED; EXCEPTIONS

Sec. 2

(a) (1) No person may acquire or possess any firearm, stun gun, or taser within this State without having in his or her possession a Firearm Owner's Identification Card previously issued in his or her name by the Department of State Police under the provisions of this Act.

(2) No person may acquire or possess firearm ammunition within this State without having in his or her possession a Firearm Owner's Identification Card previously issued in his or her name by the Department of State Police under the provisions of this Act.

430 ILCS 65/12

Sec. 12

The provisions of this Act shall not apply to the passing or transfer of any firearm or firearm ammunition upon the death of the owner thereof to his heir or legatee or to the passing or transfer of any firearm or firearm ammunition incident to any legal proceeding or action until 60 days after such passing or transfer.

The defendant was cited for Unlawful Use of Weapons and a violation of the Firearm Owners Identification Card Act. The defendant entered pleas of not guilty. The following is a transcript of a portion of the court trial.

ONCE COURT CONVENED, THE FOLLOWING EVIDENCE WAS PRESENTED:

PRESENT: JUDGE
COURT CLERK
BAILIFF
ASSISTANT STATE'S ATTORNEY
COUNSEL FOR DEFENDANT
DEFENDANT
WITNESS – OFFICER

THE COURT: The prosecution may call its first witness.

ASSISTANT STATE'S ATTORNEY: The People call the officer to the stand.

CLERK: Raise your right hand. Do you swear to tell the truth, the whole truth, and nothing but the truth, so help you God?

WITNESS: I do.

THE COURT: Please be seated.

TESTIMONY OF STATE'S WITNESS – DIRECT EXAMINATION

BY: ASSISTANT STATE'S ATTORNEY

Q: Please state your name and where you're employed.

A: Pat McGillicuddy. I'm a patrol officer with the Columbia City Police Department.

Q: How long have you served as a patrol officer with the Columbia City Police?

A: I just had my three-year anniversary.

Q: I would like to direct your attention to the first of last month. Were you on duty that day?

A: Yes, we work twelve-hour shifts so I worked until 3:00 A.M. on the first.

Q: At about 2:30 on the morning of the first, what was your location?

A: I was in my patrol car, which was parked in the lot of the convenience store located at the intersection of Center and Highland Streets in Columbia City. I was observing traffic in the area and had been watching as patrons left Jody's Bar and Grill.

Q: In what County and State is that intersection located?

A: Columbia County, Illinois.

Q: At about 2:30 A.M., what, if anything, did you observe?

A: I observed a white 2012 Honda Civic Si pulling out of the parking lot at Jody's.

Q: What was it about this vehicle that drew your attention?

A: Well, at that time of the morning, there was no other traffic in the area. When I looked at the vehicle, I noticed something hanging from the car's rear view mirror. As the car drove through the intersection I determined it was one of those tree-shaped air fresheners. That is a violation of Illinois law, 625 ILCS 5/12-503(c).

Q: What did you do then?

A: I activated my overhead lights and siren and stopped the vehicle.

Q: More specifically, where was the vehicle stopped?

A: Just south of the railroad tracks on Center Street.

Q: Did you contact the driver of the vehicle once it was stopped?

A: Yes, I did.

Q: Do you see the driver of the vehicle in the courtroom today?

A: Yes, I do.

Q: Would you please point to the person and identify some article of clothing they are wearing?

A: That is the person, seated over there [*points and describes article of clothing*].

Q: Let the record reflect the officer has identified the defendant.

THE COURT: The record will so reflect.

Q: Officer, was there anyone else in the vehicle besides the driver?

A: No, there was not.

Q: Did you have a conversation with the driver?

A: Yes, I did.

Q: To the best of your recollection, what did you say to the defendant and what did the defendant say to you?

A: I asked the defendant whether they knew it is a violation of State law to have anything hanging from the car's rear view mirror that can obstruct their vision.

Q: Did the defendant respond?

A: Yes, the response was they were unaware of the law.

Q: What did you do then?

A: I asked to see a driver's license, proof of insurance and registration for the vehicle.

Q: What happened next?

A: The driver turned on the car's interior light then leaned over and opened the glove compartment stating the documents were inside.

Q: Then what happened?

A: Once the glove compartment was opened, I observed a handgun inside.

Q: What did you do then?

A: I drew my service weapon and ordered the defendant to put his hands on the wheel. I then opened the driver's side door and ordered the defendant to step outside of the vehicle.

Q: What happened next?

A: I informed the defendant I was cuffing him for his protection as well as mine, and ordered he remain seated on the curb. I then seized the weapon and a box of ammunition from the glove compartment.

Q: Did you determine the type of weapon found in the glove box?

A: Yes, it was a 1940 9mm German Luger.

Q: What observations did you make?

A: The gun had a 4-inch barrel with a magazine holding five rounds. The ammo box was marked 124-grain Full Metal Jacket and contained 45 rounds.

Q: What did you do then?

A: I asked the defendant if he had a Firearm Owners Identification Card, or FOID, as required by State law.

Q: How did the defendant respond?

A: The defendant said, "No" and went on to state the gun was for protection. Evidently the defendant is a bartender at Jody's Bar & Grill and drives home down 10th Street, which goes through a high-crime area of the City.

Q: What did you do then?

A: I placed the defendant under arrest for the misdemeanor offenses of unlawful possession of a weapon and for no valid FOID. I secured the gun and the ammo in my patrol vehicle until turning it over to the evidence technician at the station at the end of my shift.

Q: Your Honor, the People wish to have this gun marked as People's Exhibit #1 for identification. We note for the record the weapon is unloaded and has been secured so it is not currently in firing condition.

[*The bailiff takes the gun from the Assistant State's Attorney and hands it to the court's clerk who marks it as People's Exhibit #1 for identification.*]

THE COURT: Bailiff, would you please hand what has been marked as People's Exhibit #1 for identification to defense counsel for examination before handing it to the witness. You may proceed, counsel.

Q: Officer, you are being handed People's Exhibit #1 for identification. Do you recognize this?

A: Yes, it is the gun I seized from the glove compartment of the defendant's vehicle.

Q: How do you know?

A: The gun is tagged with the case number and other identifying information. I retrieved it myself from the Department's evidence tech this morning before coming to court.

Q: Does the weapon appear to be in substantially the same condition as when you seized it from the defendant's vehicle?

A: Yes, other than the fact that the magazine has been removed and it has been secured for court, it looks the same.

ASSISTANT STATE'S ATTORNEY: Your Honor, the People ask that Exhibit #1 be admitted into evidence.

THE COURT: Defense counsel, any objection?

DEFENSE COUNSEL: No, no objection.

THE COURT: Okay, then. People's Exhibit #1 is admitted. Proceed, counsel.

Q: Officer, what, if anything, did you do to confirm the defendant did not possess a valid FOID?

A: In response to my request to the Illinois State Police to search their records for a card in the defendant's name, I received confirmation that no such card existed at the time of the stop.

ASSISTANT STATE'S ATTORNEY: Your Honor, the People ask that this document from the State indicating the defendant did not have an FOID on the date in question be marked as People's Exhibit #2. Since it is a certified record from the State we ask that it be admitted into evidence at this time.

[*The bailiff takes the document from the Assistant State's Attorney and hands it to the court's clerk who marks it as People's Exhibit #2. The Exhibit is then handed to defense counsel.*]

DEFENSE COUNSEL: I have no objection to the document being admitted into evidence, Your Honor.

THE COURT: Very well. People's Exhibit #2 is a certified document and as such, speaks for itself. It will be admitted. Anything further, counsel?

ASSISTANT STATE'S ATTORNEY: No, Your Honor, I have no further questions for the witness.

THE COURT: Defense counsel, do you wish to cross-examine the witness?

DEFENSE COUNSEL: Yes, thank you, Your Honor.

CROSS EXAMINATION OF WITNESS

BY: DEFENSE COUNSEL

Q: Officer, your testimony reflects the full extent of the conversation you had with client, is that correct?

A: Yes.

Q: You did not inquire as to where my client had obtained this gun, did you.

A: No.

Q: You did not inquire as to how long my client had been in possession of this gun, did you.

A: No.

Q: You have not conducted a recent check with the Illinois State Police to determine whether my client has obtained a FOID, have you.

A: No.

Q: I have no further questions for the officer.

THE COURT: Very well. Does the prosecutor have any questions on re-direct?

ASSISTANT STATE'S ATTORNEY: No, Your Honor. The People rest.

THE COURT: Very well. Defense counsel, do you wish to present any evidence?

Q: Yes, Your Honor, I call the defendant to the stand. My client wishes to affirm.

CLERK: Do you affirm that the information that you are about to give is the whole truth, and nothing but the truth?

DEFENDANT: I do.

THE COURT: Please be seated. Do you understand you have a Fifth Amendment right against self-incrimination that continues throughout this trial?

DEFENDANT: Yes, Your Honor.

THE COURT: Do you understand that after you answer questions posed to you by your attorney that you may be cross-examined by the prosecutor?

DEFENDANT: Yes, Your Honor.

THE COURT: Do you still wish to testify?

DEFENDANT: I do, Your Honor.

THE COURT: Counsel, you may proceed.

TESTIMONY OF DEFENSE WITNESS—DIRECT EXAMINATION

Q: Please state your name for the record.

A: [*states name*]

Q: Where do you reside?

A: I live at 10th and Clark Street in Columbia City, Illinois.

Q: How long have you lived there?

A: I just moved to Columbia City three months ago from out of state.

Q: Are you employed?

A: Yeah, as soon as I moved here, I got a bartending job at Jody's Bar & Grill. I work mostly nights—we close at 2:00 A.M.

Q: Do you recall the morning you were stopped by Officer McGillicuddy?

A: Oh yeah, it scared me half to death to get pulled over by a cop, and then to have a gun drawn on me. Yeah, I remember.

Q: Did you have a gun in your car that morning?

A: Well, yeah, actually, I did. But I can explain. See, my grandfather had just passed away and I inherited the Luger from him. I guess he got it when he was in the war. Since I moved here from a state where guns don't have to be registered or anything, I really wasn't aware of the whole FOID thing. Also, not being from around here, it turned out I moved to a pretty bad part of the City. People are getting mugged there all the time. I felt I needed the gun for protection.

ASSISTANT STATE'S ATTORNEY: Objection, Your Honor. Is there a question here? The defendant seems to be giving a narrative.

THE COURT: Counsel, if you would please ask a question.

Q: Okay, when did your grandfather die?

A: He passed just a week before I got stopped. I remember because I had just gotten back to the City after attending his funeral and visiting family for a couple of days. That's when I got the gun and the box of ammunition. He left me the gun in his will.

Q: What was your grandfather's name?

A: Franklin J. Stankowski.

DEFENSE COUNSEL: Your Honor, in accordance with Illinois Rules of Evidence, Rule 201, I ask the court to take judicial notice of the date of death of my client's grandfather. In support, I offer this copy of the decedent's obituary printed in the newspaper just six days prior to the stop in which my client is listed as a survivor. The obituary is also available online.

THE COURT: Bailiff, let me see that. Let's have this marked as Defense Exhibit A. Very well. Since the information does not appear subject to reasonable dispute, the court will take judicial notice of the fact the defendant's grandfather, Franklin J. Stankowski, died just seven days prior to his arrest. Proceed.

DEFENSE COUNSEL: Your Honor, next I would like to have this marked as Defense Exhibit B. It is a copy of Mr. Stankowski's will in which he bequeaths the Lugar to my client. Since this is a certified copy of the will from the Clerk of the Court's Office where Mr. Stankowski last lived, I ask that it be admitted at this time.

THE COURT: Very well. Anything else?

DEFENSE COUNSEL: No further questions, Your Honor.

THE COURT: Does the prosecution wish to cross-examine?

ASSISTANT STATE'S ATTORNEY: No, Your Honor. We have no questions.

THE COURT: Does the defense have anything else?

DEFENSE COUNSEL: No, Your Honor, the defense rests.

THE COURT: Does the prosecution have any rebuttal?

ASSISTANT STATE'S ATTORNEY: No, Your Honor.

THE COURT: Very well. We will now recess and upon return counsel may make their arguments before the court issues it's ruling.

BAILIFF: All rise.

ILLINOIS STATE POLICE
Springfield, Illinois

Firearm Owner's Identification Division

CERTIFIED ABSTRACT

Pursuant to the request of Officer Pat McGillicuddy, Columbia City Police Department, a search was conducted of Illinois State Police records of names of those who hold a valid Firearm Owner's Identification (FOID) Card for the following individual on the following date:

*[Defendant's name]

*[Date of arrest]

RESULTS:

The above-named individual, on the date in question, did not hold a valid Firearm Owner's Identification Card.

People's Exhibit

#2

Admitted______

Signed: *Director of State Police*
430 ILCS 65/15b

Statute

ILLEGAL POSSESSION OF ALCOHOL

625 ILCS 5/11-502 TRANSPORTATION OR POSSESSION OF ALCOHOLIC LIQUOR IN A MOTOR VEHICLE

(a) Except as provided in paragraph(c), no driver may transport, carry, possess or have any alcoholic liquor within the passenger area of any motor vehicle upon a highway in this State except in the original container and with the seal unbroken.

(b) Except as provided in paragraph(c), no passenger may carry, possess or have any alcoholic liquor within any passenger area of any motor vehicle upon a highway in this State except in the original container and with the seal unbroken.

(c) This Section shall not apply to the passengers in a limousine when it is being used for purposes for which a limousine is ordinarily used, the passengers on a chartered bus when it is being used for purposes for which chartered buses are ordinarily used or on a motor home or mini motor home as defined in Section 1-145.01 of this Code. However, the driver of any such vehicle is prohibited from consuming or having any alcoholic liquor in or about the driver's area. Any evidence of alcoholic consumption by the driver shall be prima facie evidence of such driver's failure to obey this Section. For the purposes of this Section, a limousine is a motor vehicle of the first division with the passenger compartment enclosed by a partition or dividing window used in the for-hire transportation of passengers and operated by an individual in possession of a valid Illinois driver's license of the appropriate classification pursuant to Section 6-104 of this Code.

(d) (Blank.)

(e) Any driver who is convicted of violating subsection (a) of this Section for a second or subsequent time within one year of a similar conviction shall be subject to suspension of driving privileges as provided in paragraph 23 of subsection (a) of Section 6-206 of this Code.

(f) Any driver, who is less than 21 years of age at the date of the offense and who is convicted of violating subsection (a) of this Section or a similar provision of a local ordinance, shall be subject to the loss of driving privileges as provided in paragraph 13 of subsection (a) of Section 6-205 of this Code and paragraph 33 of subsection (a) of Section 6-206 of this Code.

Statutes

UNCLASSIFIED OFFENSES

730 ILCS 5/5-5-2 UNCLASSIFIED OFFENSES

(a) The particular classification of each felony is specified in the law defining the felony. Any unclassified offense which is declared by law to be a felony or which provides a sentence to a term of imprisonment for one year or more shall be a Class 4 felony.

(b) The particular classification of each misdemeanor is specified in the law or ordinance defining the misdemeanor.

1. Any offense not so classified which provides a sentence to a term of imprisonment of less than one year but in excess of 6 months shall be a Class A misdemeanor.
2. Any offense not so classified which provides a sentence to a term of imprisonment of 6 months or less but in excess of 30 days shall be a Class B misdemeanor.
3. Any offense not so classified which provides a sentence to a term of imprisonment of 30 days or less shall be a Class C misdemeanor.

(c) Any unclassified offense which does not provide for a sentence of imprisonment shall be a petty offense or a business offense.

PETTY OFFENSE

730 ILCS 5/5-1-17 PETTY OFFENSE

"Petty offense" means any offense for which a sentence to a fine only is provided.

The defendant was charged with the petty offense of possession of alcohol. The defendant entered a plea of not guilty. The following is a transcript of a portion of the trial.

ONCE COURT CONVENED, THE FOLLOWING EVIDENCE WAS PRESENTED:

PRESENT: JUDGE
COURT CLERK
BAILIFF
ASSISTANT STATE'S ATTORNEY
COUNSEL FOR DEFENDANT
DEFENDANT
WITNESS – OFFICER PAT WALKER

THE COURT: The prosecution may call its first witness.

ASSISTANT STATE'S ATTORNEY: The People call the officer to the stand.

CLERK: Raise your right hand. Do you swear to tell the truth, the whole truth, and nothing but the truth, so help you God?

WITNESS: I do.

THE COURT: Please be seated.

TESTIMONY OF STATE'S WITNESS—DIRECT EXAMINATION

BY: ASSISTANT STATE'S ATTORNEY

Q: Please state your name and where you're employed.

A: Pat Walker, Columbia City Police Department, patrol division.

Q: Were you so employed on the first of last month?

A: Yes.

Q: At about 10:30 P.M. on that date, what was your location?

A: I was in the convenience store parking lot at the intersection of Center and Highland Streets in Columbia City.

Q: In what county and state is that located?

A: Columbia County, Illinois.

Q: What were you doing?

A: I was observing traffic at the intersection and watching patrons leave Jody's Bar and Grill.

Q: At about 10:30 P.M. on that date, what, if anything, did you observe?

A: I observed a vehicle in the northbound lane of Center Street stopped for the red light at Highland. I observed the front seat passenger take a drink from what I identified as a beer bottle.

Q: What did you do then?

A: By the time the light turned green, I activated my overhead lights and exited the parking lot, following behind the vehicle.

Q: What was the reason for the stop?

A: Violation of State law, illegal possession of alcohol.

Q: Can you describe the vehicle?

A: It was a green, 2011 Honda Civic.

Q: When you got to the vehicle, what did you see?

A: I first approached on the driver's side. The driver rolled down his window. I asked the driver for his license, registration, and proof of insurance. I observed what I believed to be a beer bottle on the floor of the vehicle between the passenger's feet.

Q: What evidence, if any, did you find that there was alcohol in the vehicle?

A: I asked the passenger, the defendant in this case, what he had there between his feet. He said 'nothing you would be interested in.' I asked to see the bottle. He handed it to me. I observed it was a bottle of Rolling Rock beer.

Q: Your Honor, the People ask that this bottle be marked as People's Exhibit #1 for identification.

THE COURT: The clerk will mark the exhibit as People's Exhibit #1 for identification and the bailiff will hand the exhibit to defense counsel to examine prior to it being handed to the witness. Proceed, counsel.

Q: Officer, you are being handed what has been marked for identification, People's Exhibit #1. Can you identify this?

A: Yes, it is an empty Rolling Rock beer bottle.

Q: Where was this bottle when you first saw it?

A: The defendant was drinking from it.

Q: More specifically, was it within the passenger compartment of the vehicle?

A: Yes, the defendant was drinking from it while seated in the passenger side of the vehicle.

Q: Is the person from whom you took this bottle in the courtroom today?

A: Yes, he is seated over there, next to his attorney.

Q: In what condition was the original seal when you obtained the bottle?

A: The cap was off, in other words, the bottle was open.

Q: Once you seized it, were you able to detect an odor about this container?

A: Oh yes, it smelled of beer.

Q: Did you conduct a test to determine whether it contained alcohol?

A: No, the bottle has the label printed right on it and it smelled of beer. It looked like beer when I poured the remaining contents of the bottle out onto the ground.

Q: Is the bottle marked People's Exhibit #1 in substantially the same condition as when you seized it from the defendant?

A: Yes.

Q: What did you do with this bottle after you seized it from the defendant?

A: I placed it in my vehicle, later turning it over to the evidence technician at the Columbia City Police Department for safekeeping.

Q: Has anyone else handled this item since you took it from the defendant?

A: Not that I know of.

ASSISTANT STATE'S ATTORNEY: Your Honor, the People ask that Exhibit #1 be admitted into evidence.

THE COURT: Defense counsel, any objection?

DEFENSE COUNSEL: Your Honor the defense objects to admission of the People's Exhibit.

THE COURT: What is the basis of your objection?

DEFENSE COUNSEL: Improper chain of custody Your Honor. May I question in aid of my objection?

THE COURT: Proceed.

DEFENSE COUNSEL: Officer, you say you seized a bottle from my client. Did you mark that bottle in any way?

A: No.

Q: Did you put a sticker on it?

A: No.

Q: Did you put your initials on it?

ASSISTANT STATE'S ATTORNEY: Objection Your Honor, the officer has already testified he did not mark the bottle in any way.

THE COURT: Sustained. Counsel for the defense, you will get your opportunity for cross-examination of this witness later. Please keep your questions limited to your objection to Exhibit #1.

DEFENSE COUNSEL: Officer, you testified that you handed this supposed bottle over to the Evidence Technician at the Columbia City Police Department?

A: Yes, that's what I said. . . .

Q: When did you next see this bottle marked People's Exhibit #1?

A: In anticipation of coming to court today, I had asked the Evidence Tech to leave the bottle out for me so I could pick it up when I finished my shift early this morning.

DEFENSE COUNSEL: Thank you, Officer. Your Honor the defense renews its objection to admission of People's Exhibit #1. The People have not presented evidence of the whole chain with regard to this bottle. We have not heard from the

Evidence Technician or anyone else who may have had the care and custody of this bottle.

THE COURT: I am going to sustain the objection for now. The prosecutor may wish to present more foundation and move to admit the exhibit at a later time.

ASSISTANT STATE'S ATTORNEY: Thank you, Your Honor. Officer, did you have a conversation with the defendant once the vehicle was stopped?

A: Yes.

Q: Who else was present during that conversation?

A: The driver of the vehicle.

Q: What did the defendant tell you?

DEFENSE COUNSEL: Objection; calls for hearsay.

THE COURT: Does the prosecution have a response?

ASSISTANT STATE'S ATTORNEY: Your Honor the statement solicited from the witness is a well-recognized exception to the Hearsay Rule. Rule 804(b)(3) of the Rules of Evidence allows the officer, in this case, to testify to the statements the defendant made against his own interest.

THE COURT: Objection overruled. Officer, if you remember the question, you may answer it.

A: I believe I had been asked what the defendant had told me. Well, as I already testified, when I first asked the defendant what that was between his feet, he told me it was nothing I'd be interested in. After asking for the bottle and receiving it from the defendant, I asked him what was in it. He told me to figure it out for myself. I told the defendant I would have no problem doing that. I poured the contents out onto the ground.

Q: What, if anything, did you observe when you poured the contents of the bottle onto the ground?

A: There was foam.

Q: Did you observe anything else within the vehicle?

A: Yes, there was a cardboard carton containing five bottles of Rolling Rock beer.

Q: What, if anything, did you do with those five bottles of beer?

A: Nothing. I noted that the bottles were cold, but their seals were not broken and both the driver and the passenger were over the age of 21.

Q: What did you do next?

A: I had requested the dispatcher to run a check on both the passenger and the driver of the vehicle. I was informed that the driver had two outstanding warrants; one from Columbia County for Failure to Appear for court, and another for burglary from the State of Pennsylvania. I then placed the driver under arrest, issued a citation to the passenger for illegal possession of alcohol, and impounded the vehicle.

ASSISTANT STATE'S ATTORNEY: Your Honor, I have no further questions for this witness.

THE COURT: Counsel for the defendant, you may cross-examine the witness.

DEFENSE COUNSEL: Officer, you can't say for sure that the bottle marked People's Exhibit #1 is the exact bottle you testified to taking from my client's possession, now can you?

A: Well, it sure looks like it. . . .

Q: Officer, please answer the question "yes" or "no."

A: No.

Q: You didn't conduct any sort of a test on the contents of the bottle, did you?

A: No.

Q: A test would have aided in your investigation, would it not?

A: No.

Q: How could a test not have been an aid to you?

A: I know a beer when I see one . . . when I smell one.

Q: Oh, I see. Do you drink a lot, Officer?

A: Well, not a lot . . . well, what I mean is, as part of my job, I have seen a lot of people under the influence of alcohol and who have been in possession of, and consuming beer. So, I think I know a beer when I see one, smell one.

Q: My client never admitted to consuming alcohol that night, did he?

A: No.

Q: My client never admitted that he was consuming beer in that vehicle that night, did he?

A: No.

Q: My client never admitted that he was in possession of an open beer that night, did he?

A: No.

Q: You never did seize the other five bottles you say you observed in the vehicle that night, did you?

A: No. They were listed as part of an inventory after the vehicle was impounded, but not seized.

Q: Officer, have you ever consumed a bottle of Rolling Rock?

A: Why, yes I have.

Q: Does the bottle marked People's Exhibit #1 look any different compared to any bottle of Rolling Rock beer that you would have consumed?

A: Well, no, I guess not.

Q: There were no fingerprints taken from this bottle marked as Exhibit #1, were there?

A: No.

Q: If there had been fingerprints taken, and they matched my client's prints, that would have aided your investigation, wouldn't it?

A: Well, yes, I guess so.

Q: Officer, you attended the Police Officer's Training Academy, didn't you? You do know how to lift fingerprints, don't you?

ASSISTANT STATE'S ATTORNEY: Objection, argumentative.

THE COURT: Overruled. This is cross-examination, counsel; I'll allow it.

DEFENSE COUNSEL: Never mind; I withdraw the question. I have no further questions for this witness.

THE COURT: The prosecution may call its next witness.

ASSISTANT STATE'S ATTORNEY: The People have no further witnesses Your Honor. We rest.

THE COURT: Defense counsel, how do you wish to proceed?

DEFENSE COUNSEL: Your Honor, the defense makes an oral Motion for Acquittal.

THE COURT: Very well. I will now issue my ruling.

TRIAL TRANSCRIPT EXERCISE

NAME ____

COURSE ____

DATE ____

Indicate the assigned trial transcript:

_____Unlawful Possession of a Weapon
_____ Illegal Possession of Alcohol

Please provide full and complete responses to the following questions:

1. What are the elements of the offense(s) with which the defendant has been charged?

2. Prior to testifying, did the witness take an oath or affirmation? What is the difference between the two?

3. Looking at the transcript, how do the questions posed by the attorney on direct examination differ from those asked on cross-examination?

4. What role did the Fifth Amendment right to counsel, or *Miranda*, have on the evidence presented at trial?

5. Identify the members of the courtroom work group involved in this trial. What is the role of each?

6. Criminal defendants are presumed innocent throughout the trial. List the evidence presented by the prosecution to rebut that presumption.

7. What is the standard of proof by which the prosecution must prove a criminal defendant guilty? Did the prosecutor meet that burden on all, or any, of the elements of the crime? State your reasoning.

8. In this case, the defendant waived a jury trial, meaning the verdict of guilty or not guilty will be issued by the judge. How would the judge's role differ if this case were being tried before a jury?

9. What are rules of evidence? What purpose do they serve in a trial? How did the rules of evidence impact this case?

10. What is the maximum penalty facing a defendant convicted of this offense? Does the penalty seem to fit the crime?

A Petition has been filed in Juvenile Court charging 11-year-old Garth Ames with disorderly conduct which is classified as a misdemeanor offense. The minor respondent has denied the allegation. The following is a transcript from the juvenile's trial.

ONCE COURT CONVENED, THE FOLLOWING EVIDENCE WAS PRESENTED:

PRESENT: JUDGE
CLERK
BAILIFF
ASSISTANT STATE'S ATTORNEY
PUBLIC DEFENDER
MINOR RESPONDENT
WITNESS – ROBERT WEEKS

BAILIFF: All rise. Court is now in session.

THE COURT: Please be seated. The State's Attorney's Office filed a petition with this court alleging that the minor, Garth Ames, is a delinquent having committed the offense of disorderly conduct in violation of 720 ILCS 5/26-1(a)(1). The minor respondent appeared previously in this court represented by the Public Defender's Office and entered a plea of not guilty and requested a trial before the court. The trial is scheduled for today. Counsel, are you ready?

PUBLIC DEFENDER: Yes, Your Honor.

ASSISTANT STATE'S ATTORNEY: The People are ready Your Honor.

THE COURT: Before we get underway, let me check on who is present in the courtroom. I see Garth is here with his parents. Otherwise, there are no spectators. If there are no issues to be brought to the court's attention before we get started, then the prosecutor may call the first witness.

ASSISTANT STATE'S ATTORNEY: The People call Bobby Weeks.

THE COURT: Bailiff, would you please escort Bobby Weeks into the courtroom? Please come in Bobby and stand before my clerk seated here to my right to be sworn in.

CLERK: Please raise your right hand . . . no your other hand, your right hand. Do you swear to tell the truth, the whole truth, and nothing but the truth, so help you God?

WITNESS: Sure.

THE COURT: Bobby, please come over here and sit in this chair on my left.

TESTIMONY OF STATE'S WITNESS – DIRECT EXAMINATION

BY: ASSISTANT STATE'S ATTORNEY

Q: Please tell us your full name and where you live.

A: Robert Sherman Weeks, but people call me Bobby. I live in Columbia City.

Q: How old are you Bobby?

A: My birthday was last week. Now I'm nine.

Q: Okay, Bobby. Did you play for a softball team here in Columbia City, Illinois?

A: Yeah, I played right field for the Columbia Prairie Dogs in the summer.

Q: Bobby, I would like you to think back to the last game of the season. What happened towards the end of the game?

A: I struck out. Well, I struck out three times. But, in the bottom of the last inning, the Prairie Dogs had bases loaded and we were only down by one. The two guys batting before me grounded out. I guess I was swinging at high pitches, but I struck out again.

Q: Okay. So the Prairie Dogs lost the game. Then what happened?

A: So I walked over to our bench to pick up my glove and my cap when Garth came up to me.

Q: Are you referring to Garth Ames who is present here in the courtroom?

A: Yeah, that's him sitting over there at that table. [Pointing.]

Q: What happened once Garth approached you after the game?

A: He started yelling at me for being so stupid. He was so mad that spit was coming out of his mouth as he was yelling.

Q: What kinds of things do you remember Garth saying to you?

A: Oh, he was saying things like I swing like a baby. He was calling me a momma's boy. He called me worthless and said I couldn't hit nothing, stuff like that.

Q: Now how close was Garth to you when he was saying these things?

A: Well, he had been watching the game. His brother Lance plays first base for the Prairie Dogs. So right after I struck out Garth came running at me. He got right up in my face.

Q: What else do you remember about that incident?

A: Well, he started kicking dirt on my shoes and said, come on, see if you can hit me. He said stuff like take a swing at me, why don't you? He said, see if you can hit me. And then, he called me a little baby again.

Q: Bobby, how did you feel while this was going on?

A: Well, I really thought he was going to punch me, or something. I was really pretty scared.

Q: Did you think about taking a swing at Garth?

A: Oh no. I guess that's what he wanted me to do, but then. . . .

PUBLIC DEFENDER: Objection to the speculation about what my client wanted.

THE COURT: Bobby, just listen carefully to the question asked of you and respond only to that question. Proceed, counsel.

ASSISTANT STATE'S ATTORNEY: So Bobby, why didn't you swing at Garth?

A: Because I knew he could beat me into the ground.

Q: Bobby do you know how long Garth was yelling at you like that?

A: Oh I don't know. It seemed like maybe ten minutes but I suppose it wasn't that long.

Q: Bobby do you know if anyone else could see or hear what was going on?

A: Oh sure. My coach was standing right there and so were a bunch of parents.

Q: Did anyone come to your assistance?

A: No, not for a long time. I could see the Prairie Dogs were leaving the park and then finally Coach told Garth to like just walk it off.

Q: What did you do then?

Q: I rode my bike home. My mom asked me what was wrong, and I told her what had happened. She hates Garth's family, so she called the cops.

Q: When you talked to the police, did you tell the officer the same things you have told the judge here today?

A: Yeah, I told the truth.

Q: You have testified under oath here today. Do you know what could happen to you if you did not tell the truth?

A: Well, I suppose I could get in trouble. But I did tell the truth.

ASSISTANT STATE'S ATTORNEY: No further questions Your Honor.

THE COURT: Very well, the defense may cross-examine.

PUBLIC DEFENDER: Well Your Honor, I do not have questions for the witness. My client pretty much agrees with the testimony that has been presented. At this time, however, we would like to make a motion for dismissal of the petition.

THE COURT: What is the basis for such motion?

PUBLIC DEFENDER: As outlined in my written motion, my contention is that the state disorderly conduct statute is unconstitutionally vague and violates the due process rights of my client under the Fifth and Fourteenth Amendments of the U.S. Constitution. As the law is written, my client could not be expected to understand that his actions were unreasonable or unlawful. The wording of the statute does not provide sufficient notice of what conduct is illegal.

THE COURT: Has the prosecutor received a copy of this motion?

ASSISTANT STATE'S ATTORNEY: Just now, Your Honor.

THE COURT: Do the People have a position on this motion?

ASSISTANT STATE'S ATTORNEY: The People understand that our laws must be clearly defined. We firmly believe that a law must provide notice to individuals of what conduct constitutes a violation. We are cognizant of the fact that a vague law may provide too much discretion to police, judges, and juries. We also recognize that a vaguely defined law may have a chilling effect on the actions of individuals who are unsure of what behavior may be considered against the law. However, it is our position that the minor respondent's rights were not violated.

THE COURT: Very well. Under the circumstances, do the People wish to call any other witnesses?

ASSISTANT STATE'S ATTORNEY: No. The People rest.

THE COURT: Am I correct in understanding the defense does not intend to call witnesses?

PUBLIC DEFENDER: That's correct. The Defense rests but would like a ruling on the motion.

THE COURT: Very well. The court will retire to chambers to consider the motion.

BAILIFF: All rise. Court will be in recess.

ONCE COURT RECONVENED, THE FOLLOWING TOOK PLACE:

THE COURT: Okay, we are once again on the record and the parties are present. The elements portion of the state disorderly conduct statute at issue reads, "A person commits disorderly conduct when he knowingly (1) Does any act in such unreasonable manner as to alarm or disturb another and to provoke a breach of the peace."

Defense counsel contends the statute, as drafted, is so vague that it violates the Constitution of the United States by providing insufficient notice of what conduct is prohibited, and that the law violates his client's due process rights.

There have been many challenges to disorderly conduct statutes that courts have decided over the years. There is a strong presumption that a law, as drafted, is constitutional. The challenger has the burden of establishing beyond a reasonable doubt that an individual of ordinary intelligence would not understand what is required of them under the law.

Other courts in this jurisdiction have previously addressed the constitutionality of this portion of the disorderly conduct statute. This court will follow *stare decisis* and will stand by prior decisions and will not disturb what are now settled points of law. Illinois courts have held the statute is not unconstitutionally vague even though the term "unreasonable" is not defined and that due process is not violated.

The court finds the defense has not met its burden and will deny the motion dismissing the petition. Since the motion has been denied, the court will now address the question of whether the minor is delinquent based upon the testimony previously presented.

DISORDERLY CONDUCT EXERCISE

NAME ____

COURSE ____

DATE ____

Please provide full and complete responses to the following five questions:

1. There are some differences in the due process rights possessed by juveniles and adults. Terminology used in the juvenile court system also differs from adult court. What distinctions between juvenile and adult court can you identify from this transcript?

2. The judge noted for the record those present in the courtroom before the trial started. Access to juvenile records is restricted. Why does the law provide for that restriction?

3. At nine years of age, is Bobby competent to testify at this trial? What factors can you identify that support your position?

4. If you were the judge, would you have found the statute unconstitutional? State your reasoning. Should a juvenile be held to the same standard as an adult when it comes to understanding the language of a law?

5. If you were the judge, would you find Garth guilty or not guilty? State your reasoning.

PART IV

SENTENCING

KEY TERMS		
aggravation	parole	restitution
goals of sentencing	plea agreement	sentencing hearing
good conduct	presentence investigation	sex offender registry
jail	prison	shock incarceration
mitigation	probation	victim impact statement

INTRODUCTION

People v. Crude

Since Max Crude was released from jail, his life has begun to change in many ways he did not anticipate. Due to the amount of time Max spent in jail prior to posting bond, his employer fired him. Unable to secure another position, Max could no longer afford the rent on his apartment and moved back in with his parents. Max has met several times with his public defender to discuss his case. His public defender has met with the prosecutor handling the case, and an agreement has been reached. Max will appear in court two more times—to change his plea and then be sentenced on the charge of Criminal Sexual Assault. You have the opportunity to sit through these hearings with Max. His life is about to take another drastic change. Will Max serve time in prison? Will he remain in the community under the supervision of a probation officer? You can decide his fate.

To further assist you in understanding the goals of sentencing, you may consider the misdemeanor and felony sentencing exercises provided. For each scenario you may determine whether the defendant should be incarcerated and, if so, the length of time to be served. Or, if the defendant is to be released to the community, with what terms and conditions must they comply?

GUILTY PLEAS

Illinois Supreme Court Rules, Rule 402, outlines for the court certain restrictions with which the court must comply when accepting a guilty plea on a criminal charge. Rule 402 is provided for your review so you are aware of what to look for when reading the transcript of the hearing in which Max Crude enters his guilty plea.

SENTENCING HEARING

Note that following acceptance of Crude's guilty plea on the felony charge, the court ordered preparation of a Presentence Investigation report. Such a report will be ordered for the sentencing hearing in most felony cases. An employee of the probation department will prepare the report for the Court. Copies of the report will be provided to defense counsel and the prosecutor to review prior to the sentencing hearing.

At the sentencing hearing, the prosecution and the defense will generally make a recommendation to the judge as to what they think would be an appropriate sentence. The judge will consider these recommendations, but the decision rests with the court. The judge will fashion a sentence that the judge deems appropriate given that particular defendant and that particular offense. Generally, on a felony charge, the judge will have the option of sentencing the defendant to serve a number of years in the custody of the Department of Corrections (the DOC will then determine the appropriate placement for the defendant), or may suspend the sentence and place the defendant on supervised probation for a term of years. The terms and conditions of probation may include serving time in the county jail.

GOALS OF SENTENCING

Have you ever wondered how state court judges determine what is an appropriate sentence? There are goals of criminal sentencing outlined for judges to follow. In Illinois, these goals appear in the Unified Code of Corrections. The statute has been provided in your materials for your review. Once you understand these goals, it should be apparent the priority of the goal or goals the judge considered in fashioning a particular sentence.

PROBATION

In cases where the court deems it appropriate to place the offender back in the community, terms and conditions will be imposed upon the defendant for his continued release on supervised probation. At times, you hear about judges who have been quite creative in the imposition of probation conditions. Generally, there is great discretion in setting terms of probation but the conditions should relate to the particular defendant.

In Illinois, the court also has the option of granting conditional discharge to a defendant for whom the judge does not feel a sentence of imprisonment or probation supervision is needed. The Illinois statute outlining conditions of probation and of conditional discharge have been provided to assist you in completing the exercises provided in Part IV.

SUPREME COURT RULES

Rule 402. Pleas of Guilty or Stipulations Sufficient to Convict

In hearings on pleas of guilty, or in any case in which the defense offers to stipulate that the evidence is sufficient to convict, there must be substantial compliance with the following:

(a) Admonitions to Defendant. The court shall not accept a plea of guilty or a stipulation that the evidence is sufficient to convict without first, by addressing the defendant personally in open court, informing him or her of and determining that he or she understands the following:

1. The nature of the charge;
2. The minimum and maximum sentence prescribed by law, including, when applicable, the penalty to which the defendant may be subjected because of prior convictions or consecutive sentences;
3. That the defendant has the right to plead not guilty, or to persist in that plea if it has already been made, or to plead guilty; and
4. That if he or she pleads guilty there will not be a trial of any kind, so that by pleading guilty he or she waives the right to a trial by jury and the right to be confronted with the witnesses against him or her; or that by stipulating the evidence is sufficient to convict, he or she waives the right to a trial by jury and the right to be confronted with any witnesses against him or her who have not testified.

(b) Determining Whether the Plea is Voluntary. The court shall not accept a plea of guilty without first determining that the plea is voluntary. If the tendered plea is the result of a plea agreement, the agreement shall be stated in open court. The court, by questioning the defendant personally in open court, shall confirm the terms of the plea agreement, or that there is no agreement, and shall determine whether any force or threats or any promises, apart from a plea agreement, were used to obtain the plea.

(c) Determining Factual Basis for Plea. The court shall not enter final judgment on a plea of guilty without first determining that there is a factual basis for the plea.

(d) Plea Discussions and Agreements. When there is a plea discussion or plea agreement, the following provisions, in addition to the preceding paragraphs of this rule, shall apply:

1. The trial judge shall not initiate plea discussions. Upon request by the defendant and with the agreement of the prosecutor, the trial judge may participate in plea discussions. Prior to participating in the plea discussions, the trial judge shall admonish the defendant and inquire as to the defendant's understanding of the following:

   That the defendant's attorney has requested that the trial judge participate in the conference to determine whether or not the charge(s) which is/are pending against the defendant can be resolved by a plea of guilty;

   That during the course of the conference the prosecutor will be present and advise the judge of the facts of the case as contained in the police reports or conversations with witnesses, that the defendant's attorney will also be present and will advise the judge of any information the defendant may have concerning the circumstances which led to the defendant's arrest in the case.

That without the conference, the judge would not learn about this information unless the case proceeded to trial.

That the judge will also learn whether the defendant has a prior criminal history, his or her driving record, whether the defendant has any alcohol or drug problem, the defendant's work history, family situation, and other things which would bear on what, if any punishment should be imposed upon the defendant as a result of his or her plea of guilty to one or more of these charges.

That these are things that the judge would not learn about unless the case went to trial and the defendant was found guilty.

That at the end of the conference, the judge may make a recommendation as to what an appropriate sentence would be.

That the defendant or the prosecutor is free to accept or reject the judge's recommendation. However, if the defendant rejects the judge's recommendation and he or she wishes to have a trial on the charges, the defendant may not obtain another judge solely on the basis that the judge participated in the conference and is aware of the facts and circumstances surrounding the incident as well as the defendant's background. This means that the defendant will be waiving his or her right to request a substitution of judge based upon the judge's knowledge of the case.

That knowing all of these things the defendant still wishes that the judge participate in this conference.

2. If a tentative plea agreement has been reached by the parties which contemplates entry of a plea of guilty in the expectation that a specified sentence will be imposed or that other charges before the court will be dismissed, the trial judge may permit, upon request of the parties, the disclosure to him or her of the tentative agreement and the reasons therefor in advance of the tender of the plea. At the same time the trial judge may also receive, with the consent of the defendant, evidence in aggravation or mitigation. The judge may then indicate to the parties whether he or she will concur in the proposed disposition; and if the judge has not yet received evidence in aggravation or mitigation, he or she may indicate that his or her concurrence is conditional on that evidence being consistent with the representations made. If the judge has indicated his or her concurrence or conditional concurrence, the judge shall so state in open court at the time the agreement is stated as required by paragraph (b) of this rule. If the defendant thereupon pleads guilty, but the trial judge later withdraws his or her concurrence or conditional concurrence, the judge shall so advise the parties and then call upon the defendant either to affirm or to withdraw his or her plea of guilty. If the defendant thereupon withdraws his or her plea, the trial judge shall recuse himself or herself.

3. If the parties have not sought or the trial judge has declined to give his or her concurrence or conditional concurrence to a plea agreement, the judge shall inform the defendant in open court at the time the agreement is stated as required by paragraph (b) of this rule that the court is not bound by the plea agreement, and that if the defendant

persists in his or her plea the disposition may be different from that contemplated by the plea agreement.

(e) Transcript. In cases in which the defendant is charged with a crime punishable by imprisonment in the penitentiary, the proceedings required by this rule to be in open court shall be taken verbatim, and upon order of the trial court transcribed, filed, and made a part of the common law record.

(f) Plea Discussions, Plea Agreements, Pleas of Guilty Inadmissible Under Certain Circumstances. If a plea discussion does not result in a plea of guilty, or if a plea of guilty is not accepted or is withdrawn, or if judgment on a plea of guilty is reversed on direct or collateral review, neither the plea discussion nor any resulting agreement, plea, or judgment shall be admissible against the defendant in any criminal proceeding.

The defendant previously entered pleas of not guilty to the felony offenses of Criminal Sexual Assault, Residential Burglary, and Theft. Pursuant to plea negotiations, an agreement has been reached between the prosecution and the defense to obviate the need for a trial. The following is a transcript from the defendant's hearing for change of plea.

ONCE COURT CONVENED, THE FOLLOWING EVIDENCE WAS PRESENTED:

PRESENT: JUDGE
CLERK
BAILIFF
ASSISTANT STATE'S ATTORNEY
PUBLIC DEFENDER
DEFENDANT

BAILIFF: All rise, court is now in session.

THE COURT: Please be seated. Would the clerk please call the first case on today's docket?

CLERK: *People v. Crude*, defendant Max Crude appears for a change of plea.

THE COURT: The defendant appears here today with court-appointed counsel for a change of plea, is that correct?

PUBLIC DEFENDER: That is correct, Your Honor. I understand the People have a motion.

ASSISTANT STATE'S ATTORNEY: We do Your Honor. The People have filed with the court an Amended Information in this case.

THE COURT: Yes, I have the original and a copy for the defendant in my file. Bailiff, please hand this copy of the Amended Information to the defendant for review. Proceed, counsel.

ASSISTANT STATE'S ATTORNEY: Pursuant to plea negotiations, the People move to dismiss the felony charges of Residential Burglary and Theft with the understanding that the defendant will enter a plea of guilty to Criminal Sexual Assault. There is no agreement regarding sentence.

THE COURT: Is that your understanding, Mr. Crude?

DEFENDANT: Yes.

THE COURT: Very well. Based upon the agreement between the parties, I will grant the People's motion to dismiss Count II Residential Burglary and Count III Theft conditioned upon the defendant's entering a plea of guilty to Count I Criminal Sexual Assault.

ASSISTANT STATE'S ATTORNEY: Thank you, Your Honor.

THE COURT: Would the prosecutor please provide a factual basis for the charge?

ASSISTANT STATE'S ATTORNEY: Had the case proceeded to trial, the evidence would have shown the defendant, Max Crude, on the date and at the location indicated in the Information, did commit an act of sexual penetration by the use of force or threat of force; or in the alternative, did commit an act of sexual penetration and the accused knew that Macy Morgan was unable to understand the nature of the act or was unable to give knowing consent.

THE COURT: Very well. Mr. Crude, how do you plead to the charge of Criminal Sexual Assault?

DEFENDANT: Guilty, Your Honor.

THE COURT: Mr. Crude, before I accept your plea of guilty to the charge, Supreme Court Rule 402, as well as State law, requires certain admonitions be made to you. Have you discussed with your attorney, and do you fully understand the nature of the charge against you?

DEFENDANT: Yes I have talked to my attorney extensively about this case, and I understand the charge against me.

THE COURT: Do you further understand that in this State Criminal Sexual Assault is a Class 1 felony that carries a penalty of not less than 4 and not more than 15 years in prison?

DEFENDANT: Yes, I understand what I am facing.

THE COURT: Do you understand that a conviction of Criminal Sexual Assault is one of the offenses in this State that requires registration as a sex offender?

DEFENDANT: Yes, I know.

THE COURT: Do you understand that you may persist in your previously entered plea of not guilty and a trial would be set during which the prosecutor would have to present sufficient evidence to prove you guilty beyond a reasonable doubt?

DEFENDANT: Yes.

THE COURT: Do you understand that if you plead guilty to this charge there will not be a trial of any kind? By pleading guilty, you waive the right to a trial by jury and the right to be confronted with the witnesses against you.

DEFENDANT: Yes, I understand.

THE COURT: Have you received any threats, or is anyone forcing you to change your plea?

DEFENDANT: No.

THE COURT: Have any promises been made to you, besides the plea agreement stated in open court today, to get you to change your plea?

DEFENDANT: No.

THE COURT: You understand that your attorney and the prosecutor may make sentence recommendations, but that it is up to me to impose the sentence in this case?

DEFENDANT: Yes.

THE COURT: Very well. I find the defendant has entered a knowing and voluntary plea to the charge and will accept his plea of guilty. Would the Clerk please check the court's calendar and schedule a date for sentencing?

CLERK: One month from today, Judge.

THE COURT: In accordance with State law, I shall order a Presentence Investigation be conducted and a report submitted to the court with copies to both counsel. Defense counsel, please review the report with your client prior to next month's hearing.

PUBLIC DEFENDER: I will, Your Honor.

THE COURT: Is there any reason the defendant should not remain out on bond pending the sentencing hearing?

ASSISTANT STATE'S ATTORNEY: No. The defendant has had no contact with the victim in this case and we do not consider him to be a flight risk.

THE COURT: Very well. I will continue the bond with the conditions previously imposed. If there is nothing further, you are excused Mr. Crude.

CIRCUIT COURT OF THE STATE OF ILLINOIS
FOR THE COUNTY OF COLUMBIA

The People of the State of Illinois,	)	
Plaintiff,	)	CASE NO. CF140212
v.	)	
	)	AMENDED
Max Crude, DOB 05/12/89	)	INFORMATION
Defendant.	)	

MARY M. FITZSIMMONS, State's Attorney in and for the County of Columbia, in the name and by the authority of the People of the State of Illinois, states that **MAX CRUDE** has, on or about July 3, 2014 within Columbia County committed the offense of:

COUNT I
CRIMINAL SEXUAL ASSAULT

In that **MAX CRUDE** did unlawfully, and knowingly (1) commit an act of sexual penetration by the use of force or threat of force; or, in the alternative, (2) commit an act of sexual penetration and the accused knew that the victim was unable to understand the nature of the act or was unable to give knowing consent; upon Macy Morgan, in violation of 720 ILCS 5/11-1.20 (a) (1) or (2).

RESPECTFULLY SUBMITTED this 17th day of November 2014.

MARY M. FITZSIMMONS, STATE'S ATTORNEY FOR COLUMBIA COUNTY

____

Mary M. Fitzsimmons

Statute
SENTENCING
730 ILCS 5/5-4-1 SENTENCING HEARING

(a) Except when the death penalty is sought under hearing procedures otherwise specified, after a determination of guilt, a hearing shall be held to impose the sentence.

The court may in its sentencing order approve an eligible defendant for placement in a Department of Corrections impact incarceration program. . . . The court may in its sentencing order recommend a defendant for placement in a Department of Corrections substance abuse treatment program . . . conditioned upon the defendant being accepted in a program by the Department of Corrections. At the hearing the court shall:

1. Consider the evidence, if any, received upon the trial;
2. Consider any presentence reports;
3. Consider the financial impact of incarceration based on the financial impact statement filed with the clerk of the court by the Department of Corrections;
4. Consider evidence and information offered by the parties in aggravation and mitigation;

4.5. Consider substance abuse treatment, eligibility screening, and an assessment, if any, of the defendant by an agent designated by the State of Illinois to provide assessment services for the Illinois courts;

5. Hear arguments as to sentencing alternatives;
6. Afford the defendant the opportunity to make a statement in his own behalf;
7. Afford the victim of a violent crime . . . committed by the defendant the opportunity to make a statement concerning the impact on the victim and to offer evidence in aggravation or mitigation; provided that the statement and evidence offered in aggravation or mitigation must first be prepared in writing in conjunction with the State's Attorney before it may be presented orally at the hearing. Any sworn testimony offered by the victim is subject to the defendant's right to cross-examine. . . ;
8. In cases of reckless homicide afford the victim's spouse, guardian, parents or other immediate family members an opportunity to make oral statements;
9. In cases involving a felony sex offense . . . consider the results of the sex offender evaluation. . . ; and
10. Make a finding of whether a motor vehicle was used in the commission of the offense for which the defendant is being sentenced.

(b) All sentences shall be imposed by the judge based upon his independent assessment of the elements specified above and any agreement as to sentence reached by the parties. The judge who presided at the trial or the judge who accepted the plea of guilty shall impose the sentence unless he is no longer sitting as a judge in that court. . . .

(c) In imposing a sentence for a violent crime or for an offense of operating or being in physical control of a vehicle while under the influence of alcohol, any other drug or any combination thereof, or a similar provision of a local ordinance, when such offense resulted in the personal injury to someone other than the defendant, the trial judge shall specify on the record the particular evidence, information, factors in mitigation and aggravation or other reasons that led to his sentencing determination. The full verbatim record of the sentencing hearing shall be filed with the clerk of the court and shall be a public record.

(c-2) If the defendant is sentenced to prison, other than when a sentence of natural life imprisonment or a sentence of death is imposed, at the time the sentence is imposed the judge shall state on the record in open court the approximate period of time the defendant will serve in custody according to the then current statutory rules and regulations for early release. . . . This statement is intended solely to inform the public, has no legal effect on the defendant's actual release, and may not be relied on by the defendant on appeal.

Statute
PURPOSES [GOALS OF SENTENCING]
730 ILCS 5/1-1-2

The purposes of this Code of Corrections are to:

(a) prescribe sanctions proportionate to the seriousness of the offenses and permit the recognition of differences in rehabilitation possibilities among individual offenders;
(b) forbid and prevent the commission of offenses;
(c) prevent arbitrary or oppressive treatment of persons adjudicated offenders or delinquents; and
(d) restore offenders to useful citizenship.

Statute
PROBATION CONDITIONS
730 ILCS 5/5-6-3 CONDITIONS OF PROBATION AND OF CONDITIONAL DISCHARGE

(a) The conditions of probation and of conditional discharge shall be that the person:

1. Not violate any criminal statute of any jurisdiction;
2. Report to or appear in person before such person or agency as directed by the court;
3. Refrain from possessing a firearm or other dangerous weapon;
4. Not leave the State without the consent of the court or, in circumstances in which the reason for the absence is of such an emergency nature that prior consent by the court is not possible, without the prior notification and approval of the person's probation officer. Transfer of a person's probation or conditional discharge supervision to another state is subject to acceptance by the other state pursuant to the Interstate Compact for Adult Offender Supervision;
5. Permit the probation officer to visit him at his home or elsewhere to the extent necessary to discharge his duties;
6. Perform no less than 30 hours of community service and not more than 120 hours of community service, if community service is available in the jurisdiction. . . .
7. If he or she is at least 17 years of age and has been sentenced to probation or conditional discharge for a misdemeanor or felony;

• • • • • • • • • • • • • • • • • • • •

9. If convicted of a felony, or of any misdemeanor [as designated], physically surrender at a time and place designated by the court, his or her Firearm Owner's Identification Card and any and all firearms in his or her possession. . . .

(b) The Court may in addition to other reasonable conditions relating to the nature of the offense or the rehabilitation of the defendant as determined for each defendant in the proper discretion of the Court require that the person:

1. Serve a term of periodic imprisonment . . .
2. Pay a fine and costs;
3. Work or pursue a course of study or vocational training;
4. Undergo medical, psychological or psychiatric treatment; or treatment for drug addiction or alcoholism;
5. Attend or reside in a facility established for the instruction or residence of defendants on probation;
6. Support his dependents;
7. And in addition if a minor:
   - (i) reside with his parents or in a foster home;
   - (ii) attend school;
   - (iii) attend a non-residential program for youth;
   - (iv) contribute to his own support at home or in a foster home;
   - (v) with the consent of the superintendent of the facility, attend an educational program at a facility other than the school in which the offense was committed if he or she is convicted of a crime of violence . . . committed in a school, on the real property comprising a school, or within 1,000 feet of the real property comprising a school;

8. Make restitution . . .
9. Perform some reasonable public or community service;
10. Serve a term of home confinement . . .
11. Comply with the terms and conditions of an order of protection issued by the court . . .

••

13. Contribute a reasonable sum of money, not to exceed the maximum amount of the fine authorized for the offense for which the defendant was sentenced, (i) to a "local anti-crime program" . . .
14. Refrain from entering into a designated geographic area except upon such terms as the court finds appropriate . . .
15. Refrain from having any contact, directly or indirectly, with certain specified persons or particular types of persons, including but not limited to members of street gangs and drug users or dealers;
16. Refrain from having in his or her body the presence of any illicit drug. . . .

••

STATE OF ILLINOIS

Columbia County Probation and Court Services

PRESENTENCE REPORT

Confidential

Prepared for:	The Honorable Patricia Smith Circuit Court Judge
Prepared by:	Chris Perez Probation Office for the First Judicial District
Defendant's Name:	Max Crude
Case Number:	CJ140212
Arrest Date:	July 3, 2014
SSN:	555-00-1212

DOB: May 12, 1989
Place of Birth: Columbia City, Illinois
Sex: Male
Defendant's Legal Address: 1712 Main Street, Columbia City, Illinois

OFFENSE DATA

Max Crude was arrested on July 3, 2014, and charged with the felony offenses of 1) criminal sexual assault, 2) residential burglary, and 3) theft. Bond was initially set at $100,000. Crude's bond was reduced to $10,000 two weeks later at the time of his preliminary hearing. Later that day, Crude posted bond and was released from the Columbia County Jail with conditions imposed by the court. Crude initially plead not guilty to all three charges.

Crude subsequently appeared in Circuit Court and entered a plea of guilty to criminal sexual assault pursuant to an oral plea agreement placed on the record whereby the remaining two charges were dismissed. There is no sentencing agreement between the parties. Crude remains out of custody on bond; there have been no allegations of violation of any conditions of bond. There are no holds from other courts, and no codefendants in this case or co-offenders.

OFFENSE CONDUCT

Macy Morgan currently resides in Columbia County. Morgan declined to submit an impact statement for this report indicating she will give an oral statement in open court at the sentencing hearing. Morgan has submitted to the State's Attorney's Office statements for costs incurred to date for medical and psychological treatment as a direct result of this offense.

Max Crude, through his attorney, provided a written statement regarding the offense that states: "I thought we were just having fun. I knew she had had a lot to drink but we both had. I thought she liked me as much as I liked her. After talking things over with my lawyer, I now see that I shouldn't have done what I did. If I could do it over again, I would just have taken her home. I'm really sorry if I caused a problem."

DEFENDANT'S CRIMINAL HISTORY

Crude relates he has no criminal history as an adult. As a juvenile, Crude was convicted of underage consumption of alcohol at age 16, was fined, but was not placed on probation. A computer check verifies this information. Crude has no other pending charges nor is he currently on supervision.

OFFENDER CHARACTERISTICS

Max Crude has lived his whole life in Columbia County. Crude lived with his parents, Carl and Gretchen Crude, until one year ago when Max moved to his own apartment. Crude reports that since being released from custody he has moved back to his parents' home. Crude has no siblings. Crude is presently single and has no marital history. He has never had any children.

DEFENDANT'S PHYSICAL AND MENTAL CONDITION

Physical Description
Height: 6.0
Weight: 190
Eye Color: Brown
Hair Color: Brown
Tattoos: Tombstone on chest
Scars: None

Crude is healthy and has no history of health problems.

Mental and Emotional Health
Crude has no history of mental or emotional problems, and no history of treatment for such problems.

DEFENDANT'S USE OF SUBSTANCES

Max Crude reports having used alcohol and marijuana. Crude reports he first consumed beer with his friends at age 15. He reports he would usually drink beer at parties on weekends since that age and continued to do so up until the time of his arrest. Crude began smoking marijuana at age 16. Crude reports smoking marijuana "off and on" since then, but has not used any substances since being released from jail on this charge.

MILITARY

Crude reports he has not served in the military.

EDUCATION AND TRAINING

Max Crude graduated from Columbia High School in June 2007. He has earned 15 credits from Columbia Community College, taking primarily general education classes. Crude is not currently enrolled in any educational or training program. Crude does not have any specialized skills or a professional license.

EMPLOYMENT

At the time of his arrest, Crude was employed full-time with the Columbia Park District. Crude reports he was discharged from his job because he had worked there only a short time prior to his arrest and he could not post bond for approximately two weeks. Crude reports he is currently seeking employment but that no one will hire him prior to his sentencing hearing.

Given that Crude is unemployed and has few assets, he would have difficulty paying financial obligations incurred as a result of this conviction.

SENTENCE RECOMMENDATION

In consideration of the above information, my sentence recommendation is for the defendant to serve a period of time, to be determined by the court, in a state penal institution. The court may wish to consider placing the defendant in a Department of Corrections impact incarceration program; however, the defendant may not be accepted into such a program because of the violent nature of the offense. It is further recommended that the defendant be ordered to reimburse the victim for any medical and counseling expenses incurred as a direct result of this offense. Since the defendant is unemployed and has limited resources, he will be unable to make payments towards his court-ordered financial obligations until his release from custody.

Respectfully submitted,

Chris Perez

Chris Perez, Senior Probation Officer Harold Gross, Supervisor

This report has been prepared pursuant to 730 ILCS 5/5-3-2 *and shall be filed of record with the court in a sealed envelope. The report may be disclosed only in accordance with the requirements of* 730 ILCS 5/5-3-4.

The defendant previously entered a plea of guilty to the felony offense of Criminal Sexual Assault pursuant to a plea agreement. The following is a transcript from the defendant's sentencing hearing.

ONCE COURT CONVENED, THE FOLLOWING EVIDENCE WAS PRESENTED:

PRESENT: JUDGE
CLERK
BAILIFF
ASSISTANT STATE'S ATTORNEY
PUBLIC DEFENDER
DEFENDANT
VICTIM

THE COURT: The court will next take up the sentencing hearing in the case of *People v. Crude.* Let the record reflect the parties are present. Counsel, are we ready to proceed with the hearing today?

ASSISTANT STATE'S ATTORNEY: Yes, Your Honor.

THE COURT: Mr. Crude, have you had an opportunity to review with your attorney the Presentence Investigation Report prepared in this matter?

DEFENDANT: Yes, I have.

THE COURT: Has your attorney answered any questions you may have had about the information contained in the report, or any questions you may have had regarding today's proceeding?

DEFENDANT: Yes, we have gone over everything.

THE COURT: As a matter of review, the parties entered into an agreement whereby the People dismissed the felony counts of residential burglary and theft in exchange for the defendant pleading guilty to the charge of Criminal Sexual Assault contained in the Amended Information filed in this case. The court understands there is no sentencing agreement. Is that your understanding Mr. Crude?

DEFENDANT: Yes, Judge.

THE COURT: Mr. Crude, the crime of Criminal Sexual Assault is a Class 1 felony in this state and as such carries a penalty of imprisonment for not less than 4 years and not more than 15 years. This is also an offense for which you must register with the State as a sex offender. Is that understood?

DEFENDANT: Yes.

THE COURT: Mr. Crude, do you further understand that your attorney will make a sentence recommendation to the court, as will the prosecutor, but it is up to me—it is up to the court to decide what the sentence will be. Do you have any questions for me?

DEFENDANT: No, Your Honor, I'm good.

THE COURT: Very well. Do the People intend to call any witnesses in aggravation today?

ASSISTANT STATE'S ATTORNEY: No, Judge, however, Macy Morgan is present in the courtroom and has prepared a written impact statement that we would like to submit to the court at this time. A copy has been provided to the defense.

THE COURT: Okay. Bailiff, would you please hand the document to me? Mr. Crude, have you reviewed this document with your attorney?

DEFENDANT: I have.

THE COURT: Do you have any questions or comments regarding anything contained in this statement?

DEFENDANT: No, Your Honor.

THE COURT: Very well. Does the defense intend to call any witness in mitigation?

PUBLIC DEFENDER: No, we won't be calling witnesses, but my client wishes to address the court at the appropriate time.

THE COURT: Certainly. The court will now hear the prosecution's argument and sentence recommendation.

ASSISTANT STATE'S ATTORNEY: Thank you, Your Honor. Macy Morgan had just turned 21 years old at the beginning of July. In the afternoon of July 2nd, Macy was a happy, carefree young woman who was excited about meeting an online friend that night for the first time. The defendant's violent act changed Macy forever. In the time that has passed since the attack, Macy is no longer the outgoing, spirited young woman she had been before meeting the defendant. Although Macy has been seeing a counselor since this incident, it is difficult for her to go out in public. She no longer feels she can trust people. She does not see her friends nor does she take part in family activities. Macy had to quit her summer job and is still unemployed. She was unable to continue her studies in pharmacology at

Columbia University so now her education is on hold. Macy is a shell of her former self. Macy's impact statement speaks to what she has gone through.

The defendant has no criminal history as an adult. As a juvenile, the defendant was convicted of underage drinking. According to the PSI report, it appears the defendant has had a problem with alcohol and drugs most of his life. The defendant had consumed a great deal of alcohol the night this crime occurred. But alcohol does not excuse his violent behavior.

The People recommend the court sentence the defendant to serve a term of five years imprisonment. We do not recommend the impact incarceration program for the defendant because of the violent nature of this crime. Because of the nature of the charge, it is doubtful the defendant would be accepted into the program. The People certainly do not believe the defendant should be placed on probation.

At this time, the People wish to submit to the court an itemized list of out-of-pocket expenses incurred by Macy and her family for medical and psychological counseling. Also attached to this document is a letter from Macy's counselor in which she lists anticipated counseling costs. A copy has been provided to the defense. Thank you.

THE COURT: Bailiff, if you would please hand those papers to me. Defense? You may proceed.

PUBLIC DEFENDER: Thank you. I would like to say a few words and then Max would like to address the court. I have represented a lot of individuals appearing before this court for sentencing. I have to say Max is an exception. Rarely do I see the kind of remorse that I have seen expressed by Max. On the afternoon of July 2nd, Max was a young man with great potential. He had just started a job with great promise for advancement. Max lived here in Columbia City with his parents all of his life until about a year ago when he finally moved into his own apartment near by. Max is very close to his parents. His younger sister was killed in a tragic car accident three years ago; the night she graduated from high school. Max has been a major source of comfort to his parents since her death. At Gretchen's funeral, Max vowed to make the world a better place in her honor.

Max has never had a run-in with police as an adult. He has been a good son, a good citizen. What occurred on July 2nd has been tragic for both Max and the complainant. But I beg of you, Your Honor, do not compound the tragedy by throwing this young man's life away. A prison sentence will devastate his family, taking their only remaining child away from them, and it will ruin any chance Max has for a successful future.

Your Honor, I would ask that the court consider the impact incarceration program for Max, but I agree with the prosecutor. I doubt that Max would be accepted into the program simply because of the nature of the charge. Therefore, Your Honor, I ask the court to place Max on probation so that he may remain in the community. That way Max can remain productive, have a relationship with his family, and have a positive impact on society. Your Honor, Max is willing to be supervised at the strictest level of probation. Since Max has been out of jail on bond, he has not violated any conditions of his release, including having no contact with the complainant. If Max is employed, he will be able to pay restitution and any other court-ordered financial obligations. Just last week Max found a sponsor and has been attending AA/NA meetings.

Your Honor, I ask the court to suspend any prison sentence and place Max on probation for a period of ten years. That will surely be sufficient time to prove to the court that he will not commit another violation of the law. Max?

DEFENDANT: Your Honor, I want to apologize to Macy and to my parents for what happened. What happened that night . . . it's just not the person I am. I just want to prove to the court and to everybody that nothing like this will ever happen again. I just want to . . . [sobbing].

THE COURT: Bailiff, take this box of tissues to counsel table. Counsel, would you like a few minutes while your client composes himself? Do we need to take a recess?

PUBLIC DEFENDER: No, Your Honor, after consulting with my client, he indicates that's all he has to say.

THE COURT: Very well. Does the prosecutor have anything else?

ASSISTANT STATE'S ATTORNEY: No, Your Honor, we stick with our recommendation. Granting probation would only serve to deprecate the crime that has occurred.

THE COURT: Thank you, counsel. If the defendant would please stand, I will impose sentence in this case.

People v. Crude Exercise

NAME ____

COURSE ____

DATE ____

Please provide full and complete responses to the following five questions:

1. Does it appear the judge was in compliance with applicable law when accepting Crude's guilty plea? What did you rely upon in making this determination?

2. Why do you think the law requires a judge to make these admonitions to the defendant prior to accepting his guilty plea?

3. If you were the judge, how would you sentence Max Crude? Would you follow the recommendation of the prosecutor or the recommendation of defense counsel? Which of the goals of sentencing did you consider a priority in fashioning Crude's sentence?

4. If serving time in prison were the only option, how many years do you think Crude should serve? Does the concept of "good conduct" enter into your thinking? Explain how this would further the goals of sentencing.

5. If the judge granted probation to Max Crude, what conditions of probation would you recommend be ordered? Remember that serving a jail sentence may be ordered as a condition of probation. Explain how this would further the goals of sentencing.

MISDEMEANOR SENTENCING EXERCISE

NAME ______________________________

COURSE ______________________________

DATE ______________________________

For each of the following five scenarios, imagine you are the judge who has taken the guilty plea from the defendant. Considering the goals of sentencing and the conditions of probation [730 ILCS 5/5-6-3] that may be imposed, indicate the sentence you would impose:

1. Frankie, 20 years old, has pleaded guilty to driving under the influence of alcohol. Frankie lives at home with his parents and his sister who is 17. Frankie is enrolled in a full-time program at his community college. Frankie has no prior criminal history.

2. Trudy is 25 and has entered a guilty plea to driving under the influence of alcohol. She is the mother of a six-year-old daughter (the child's father is unknown). Her family lives out of state. Trudy works as a bartender. She had a DUI six years ago for which she successfully completed probation and a 30-day private outpatient treatment program.

3. Joel, 22, has pleaded guilty to unlawful possession of alcohol (while a passenger in a friend's vehicle). Joel has just graduated college with a Bachelor's degree and has moved back in with his parents. He is currently unemployed. Joel's criminal history shows three underage drinking citations while attending college.

4. Sammie, at 19, has three prior misdemeanor theft convictions. Sammie's MO (method of operation) seems to be entering a business and grabbing merchandise just inside the door and taking off with it. Sammie has agreed to plead guilty to a misdemeanor rather than face a felony burglary charge for this incident. Sammie is neither employed or in any educational program. Sammie does not have a regular residence of his own but states he stays with friends. Sammie has appeared for sentencing wearing a T-shirt with a marijuana leaf on the front.

5. James, who is 20, has been charged under a new law that prohibits people from exposing three inches or more of their underwear. The maximum penalty is a fine not to exceed $500 and/or incarceration not to exceed 30 days in jail. James states that all of his pants are "low-slung." James has no criminal history. James works part-time at a restaurant (in the kitchen) and takes classes periodically at his community college.

FELONY SENTENCING EXERCISE

NAME ____

COURSE ____

DATE ____

For each of the following five scenarios, imagine you are the judge who has taken the guilty plea from the defendant. Considering the goals of sentencing and the conditions of probation [730 ILCS 5/5-6-3] that may be imposed, indicate the sentence you would impose:

1. Tomas is a 19-year-old convicted of aggravated battery. The victim is a 19-year-old male who was taken to the emergency room with a head wound. The staples have been removed, but the victim reports he continues to suffer severe headaches that prevent him from working. The victim does not have medical insurance. The criminal history for Tomas shows two battery convictions. Tomas is a full-time student at his community college. He is unemployed.

2. Jackson, 30, is married and has three young children at home. Jackson has pleaded guilty to stealing a HD-LCD television from a "big box" store near his home. Jackson was fired from his real estate job three months prior to the theft. His wife has not worked since their first child was born. This is Jackson's first conviction.

3. Twenty-two-year old Kim is convicted of forgery for having cashed a stolen check in the amount of $200 (which Kim states she spent on drugs). Kim is single and has two children who live with her mother. As an adult, Kim has prior convictions for possession of drug paraphernalia and possession of heroin for which she is currently on probation. Kim has not completed any drug treatment program.

4. Summer is a 22-year-old convicted of felony possession of cocaine. She has a prior conviction for possession of drug paraphernalia for which she paid a fine. Summer is single, living alone, and works full-time as a cashier.

5. Fred is a 55-year-old prisoner who has served 12 years for having sexually abused a nine-year-old neighbor girl. Fred is up for parole. Should Fred be paroled, what would you recommend as conditions of parole?

PART V

POST-SENTENCE

KEY TERMS	
admit-deny hearing	petition
conditions of probation	preponderance of the evidence
hearsay	probation revocation

INTRODUCTION

People v. Davenport

Prison? Probation? Those were two options the judge considered when sentencing Sherry Davenport for her felony theft conviction. After considering the goals of sentencing, the judge opted to place Sherry on probation for a period of two years. Sherry was ordered to comply with certain terms and conditions of probation. The judge told Sherry at her sentencing hearing that by being granted probation she, "Held the key to her cell." The judge went on to explain that if Sherry violated those conditions, her probation could be revoked and she could end up serving a term of imprisonment.

Not long after Sherry was sentenced, she ended up back in court to answer to a Petition to Revoke Probation filed by the State's Attorney's Office. Sherry denied violating the terms of her probation. A hearing was held a week later. Is Sherry noncompliant? What is the best course of action to take? You decide.

CONDITIONS OF PROBATION

In Illinois, probation means the judge has sentenced the defendant to a period of conditional release under the supervision of a probation officer. Defendants convicted of a misdemeanor or most felony offenses may be granted probation. (Probation is not to be confused with "parole," which is early release from a prison.) The defendant placed on probation will be ordered to comply with certain terms and conditions. Many of these conditions are considered standard, such as obeying all laws, and will apply to all probationers. Other conditions, such as drug or alcohol treatment, will be ordered when the court deems it appropriate.

For any observer of our criminal court system, it soon becomes clear that probation is commonly granted to those convicted of crime. The judicial decision to grant probation may be based on factors such as policy or prison and jail overcrowding. With the large numbers of defendants receiving a sentence of probation, it should not be surprising that courts also spend a good portion of time addressing alleged violations of probation.

PROBATION REVOCATION

Procedurally, should it appear to the probation officer that the conditions of probation have been violated, the State's Attorney's Office will file a Petition with the court outlining the alleged violations. While those who are convicted of a crime still possess certain rights under the Federal and State constitutions, the fact is, probationers are afforded fewer procedural safeguards than those who have not yet been convicted.

The prosecutor has the burden of proof in establishing that the probationary conditions were violated. It is significant to note, however, that the standard at such an evidentiary hearing is "preponderance of the evidence," a much lower burden than the prosecutor faces in a criminal trial. The probationer maintains the right to counsel and the right to confront and cross-examine adverse witnesses.

Should there be a determination that a probationer has violated probation, the judge must still consider the appropriate action to take. Depending upon the number or the severity of the conditions violated, the judge still has options. The court may, for example, continue probation and consider additional conditions, including jail time. For more serious violations, the judge may revoke probation and resentence the defendant. In the case of a felon, of course, that could mean imprisonment.

SUPREME COURT RULES

Rule 402A. Admissions or Stipulations in Proceedings to Revoke Probation, Conditional Discharge or Supervision.

In proceedings to revoke probation, conditional discharge or supervision in which the defendant admits to a violation of probation, conditional discharge or supervision, or offers to stipulate that the evidence is sufficient to revoke probation, conditional discharge or supervision, there must be substantial compliance with the following.

(a) Admonitions to Defendant. The court shall not accept an admission to a violation, or a stipulation that the evidence is sufficient to revoke, without first addressing the defendant personally in open court, and informing the defendant of and determining that the defendant understands the following:

1. the specific allegations in the petition to revoke probation, conditional discharge or supervision;
2. that the defendant has the right to a hearing with defense counsel present, and the right to appointed counsel if the defendant is indigent and the underlying offense is punishable by imprisonment;
3. that at the hearing, the defendant has the right to confront and cross-examine adverse witnesses and to present witnesses and evidence in his or her behalf;
4. that at the hearing, the State must prove the alleged violation by a preponderance of the evidence;
5. that by admitting to a violation, or by stipulating that the evidence is sufficient to revoke, there will not be a hearing on the petition to revoke probation, conditional discharge or supervision, so that by admitting to a violation, or by stipulating that the evidence is sufficient to revoke, the defendant waives the right to a hearing and the right to confront and cross-examine adverse witnesses, and the right to present witnesses and evidence in his or her behalf; and
6. the sentencing range for the underlying offense for which the defendant is on probation, conditional discharge or supervision.

(b) Determining Whether Admission Is Voluntary. The court shall not accept an admission to a violation, or a stipulation sufficient to revoke without first determining that the defendant's admission is voluntary and not made on the basis of any coercion or promise. If the admission or tendered stipulation is the result of an agreement as to the disposition of the defendant's case, the agreement shall be stated in open court. The court, by questioning the defendant personally in open court, shall confirm the terms of the agreement, or that there is no agreement, and shall determine whether any coercion or promises, apart from an agreement as to the disposition of the defendant's case, were used to obtain the admission.

(c) Determining Factual Basis for Admission. The court shall not revoke probation, conditional discharge or supervision on an admission or a stipulation without first determining that there is a factual basis for the defendant's admission or stipulation.

(d) Application of Rule 402. The provisions of Rules 402(d), (e), and (f) shall apply to proceedings on a petition to revoke probation, conditional discharge or supervision.

CIRCUIT COURT OF THE STATE OF ILLINOIS
FOR THE COUNTY OF COLUMBIA

The People of the State of Illinois,		)	
	Plaintiff,	)	
v.		)	
		)	CASE NO. CF14-0311
Sherry Davenport, DOB 04/01/93		)	
	Defendant.	)	

CONDITIONS OF PROBATION

The above-named defendant has been granted probation for a period of two (2) years from the date of sentencing in the above-referenced case, having been convicted of theft [720 ILCS 5/16-1]. The terms and conditions of probation are as follows:

1. Obey the laws of all jurisdictions.
2. Immediately notify your probation officer if arrested or charged with any offense.
3. Report in person to your probation officer each month as scheduled.
4. Permit your probation officer to visit you in your home or place of employment.
5. Maintain employment or pursue educational goals as agreed upon with your probation officer.
6. Do not associate with anyone deemed inappropriate by your probation officer.
7. Do not ingest, or otherwise have in your system, any alcohol or unauthorized controlled substance.
8. Do not possess, or otherwise have in your residence, any alcohol, controlled substance or drug-related paraphernalia.
9. Submit to random urinalysis testing as directed by your probation officer.
10. Submit to evaluations and successfully complete any recommended course of treatment.
11. Participate in AA/NA and any other program as recommended by your probation officer.
12. Do not leave the State of Illinois without written permission from your probation officer.
13. Complete 40 hours of community service at the direction of your probation officer.

You have been granted the privilege of probation. Should you violate any of the above-listed terms and conditions of probation, your probation officer may invoke court-approved sanctions or request the State's Attorney's Office file a petition alleging violation. Should you be found in violation of these terms and conditions, your probation may be modified or revoked. Upon revocation, the court may resentence you on the underlying charge for which you received probation.

Signed: *Sherry Davenport*

The defendant was previously convicted on a felony theft charge and was granted probation. The State's Attorney's Office has filed a Petition alleging the defendant has violated the terms and conditions of her probation. The following is a transcript from the defendant's court appearance in which she is to admit or deny the allegations.

ONCE COURT CONVENED, THE FOLLOWING TOOK PLACE:

PRESENT: JUDGE
CLERK
BAILIFF
ASSISTANT STATE'S ATTORNEY
DEFENSE COUNSEL
DEFENDANT

THE COURT: We will now take up the matter of *People v. Davenport*. The defendant appears with counsel. The State's Attorney's Office has filed a Petition in this case alleging the defendant has violated certain terms and conditions of her probation. At today's hearing, the defendant will have an opportunity to admit or deny the alleged violations. Ms. Davenport, I did not expect to see you in this court again so soon. Counsel, have you had an opportunity to review the Petition with your client?

DEFENSE COUNSEL: Yes, Judge, we have discussed it thoroughly.

THE COURT: Ms. Davenport, before I ask you to either admit or deny the allegations contained in the Petition, Supreme Court Rule 402A, as well as state law, requires that I give you certain admonitions to ensure you understand what is taking place.

DEFENDANT: Yes, Your Honor.

THE COURT: Ms. Davenport, you remember when you were sentenced in this court you were granted probation for a period of two years. On the day you were sentenced, you signed a document listing the conditions of your probation. Do you recall that?

DEFENDANT: Yes, Your Honor.

THE COURT: Have you had adequate time to discuss with your attorney the nature of the allegations against you?

DEFENDANT: I have.

THE COURT: Should you deny any or all of the allegations in the Petition, you have the right to a hearing. The prosecution would have the burden of establishing the violations by a preponderance of the evidence. That is a lower burden than the prosecution faces at a trial. However, at that hearing, your attorney may cross-examine witnesses called by the People and you may present witnesses and evidence on your own behalf. Is that understood?

DEFENDANT: Yes.

THE COURT: Ms. Davenport, if you admit to the alleged violations, there will not be a hearing. You will in effect be waiving your right to a hearing and the right to confront and cross-examine adverse witnesses and the right to present witnesses and evidence on your own behalf. Is that understood?

DEFENDANT: Yes.

THE COURT: If you admit to the allegations, or if you are found in violation of the conditions of your probation, you may be resentenced. The theft charge you were convicted of is a Class 4 felony for which you could be sentenced to serve not less than 1 year and not more than 3 years in the Department of Corrections. Is that understood?

DEFENDANT: Yes.

THE COURT: I will now go through the allegations contained in the Petition one at a time and then will ask you to either admit or deny the allegation. Do you have any questions of me?

DEFENDANT: No.

THE COURT: It is alleged you violated condition number 3 by not meeting with your probation officer at your scheduled appointment last month. Do you admit or deny?

DEFENDANT: Deny.

THE COURT: It is alleged you violated condition number 5 in that you were fired from your job for missing too many days of work. Do you admit or deny?

DEFENDANT: Deny.

THE COURT: It is alleged you violated condition number 6 in that you allowed another probationer to move into your apartment against the wishes of your probation officer. Do you admit or deny?

DEFENDANT: Deny.

THE COURT: It is alleged you violated condition number 8 in that beer was found in your refrigerator. Do you admit or deny?

DEFENDANT: Deny.

THE COURT: It is alleged you violated condition number 11 by no longer attending AA/NA meetings on a regular basis. Do you admit or deny?

DEFENDANT: Deny.

THE COURT: It is alleged you violated condition number 12 by leaving the State of Illinois without the written permission of your probation officer. Do you admit or deny?

DEFENDANT: Deny.

THE COURT: Very well. I will schedule a hearing at which time evidence may be presented on these allegations. Can the People be ready to proceed one week from today?

ASSISTANT STATE'S ATTORNEY: Yes Judge. We'll be ready.

THE COURT: If there is nothing further, then you may be dismissed.

The defendant appeared in court last week and denied violating the conditions of her probation, as alleged in the Petition filed by the State's Attorney's Office. The parties are back in court today for a presentation of evidence. The following is a transcript of the hearing.

ONCE COURT CONVENED, THE FOLLOWING EVIDENCE WAS PRESENTED:

PRESENT: JUDGE
CLERK
BAILIFF
ASSISTANT STATE'S ATTORNEY
DEFENSE COUNSEL
DEFENDANT
WITNESS – CHRIS PEREZ

THE COURT: We will now take up the case of *People v. Davenport* scheduled for an evidentiary hearing on the alleged probation violations contained in the People's Petition. I see the parties are present. If there are no preliminary matters for the court, then the prosecution may call its first witness.

ASSISTANT STATE'S ATTORNEY: Thank you. The People call Chris Perez.

THE COURT: Please stand before the clerk to be sworn and then have a seat in the witness stand.

CLERK: Raise your right hand. Do you swear to tell the truth, the whole truth, and nothing but the truth, so help you God?

WITNESS: I do.

TESTIMONY OF STATE'S WITNESS—DIRECT EXAMINATION

BY: ASSISTANT STATE'S ATTORNEY

Q: Please state your name and how you're employed.

A: Chris Perez. I'm a probation officer.

Q: Are you familiar with Sherry Davenport?

A: Yes, I have been supervising Sherry on my caseload since she was sentenced on the felony theft charge in this court.

Q: Do you recall when you first met with Ms. Davenport?

A: Yes. Actually I was present in court at the time she was sentenced. Immediately following court, I met with Sherry to go over the written conditions of her probation. Sherry stated she understood all of the conditions and then signed the document.

Q: Did you have regularly scheduled meetings set up with Ms. Davenport?

A: Yes, Sherry was to meet with me the first Monday of each month. At these meetings, we would go over her probation plan to see how she is progressing.

Q: How have those meetings been going?

A: Sherry hadn't been doing too badly. She was late a couple of times, but I thought we had that worked out. Then last month she missed her appointment entirely.

Q: What did you do?

A: I tried calling her cell phone but she didn't pick up. I thought maybe she had been called into work, so I called her employer.

Q: What did you find out?

A: Her boss told me . . .

DEFENSE COUNSEL: Objection. Hearsay.

THE COURT: Sustained.

ASSISTANT STATE'S ATTORNEY: Let me rephrase the question. Were you able to contact Ms. Davenport at work?

A: No.

Q: What did you do?

A: After my last appointment of the day, I went to Sherry's apartment.

Q: What happened once you arrived?

A: A man answered the door. I identified myself and asked for Sherry. He said . . .

DEFENSE COUNSEL: Objection. Hearsay.

THE COURT: Sustained.

ASSISTANT STATE'S ATTORNEY: Let me ask you a question. What happened after you asked for Ms. Davenport?

A: I was allowed to enter the apartment.

Q: What did you do once inside the apartment?

A: I walked around the apartment and confirmed that Sherry was not there.

Q: Then what happened?

A: As I walked into the living room, the front door opened and I saw Sherry walk in. She was carrying a suitcase and a beach bag.

Q: Did you speak with her? What did she say?

DEFENSE COUNSEL: Objection. The question calls for hearsay.

THE COURT: Overruled. The witness may answer.

A: I asked her where she had been. She told me she had been out shopping.

Q: Then what happened?

A: Sherry reached into her beach bag and removed a white paper sack. I followed her into the kitchen. Sherry opened the refrigerator and placed the bag inside. At this time I noticed several beer cans in the trash. I opened the refrigerator and observed probably a dozen unopened cans of beer inside.

Q: What did you do next?

A: I opened the white paper sack Sherry had just placed in the refrigerator. It contained a bag of cheese curds. The label on the bag was from a cheese shop located in the Wisconsin Dells.

Q: Then what did you do?

A: I went back into the living room and looked at what else was in the beach bag. I found an 8 × 10 photograph of Sherry standing next to a wooden Indian statue. I noticed that Sherry was wearing the same outfit as she had on in the photograph.

Q: Had you granted her permission to leave the state?

A: No.

Q: Then what did you do?

A: I reminded Sherry that she had missed her appointment with me and I asked her why she wasn't at work. She told me she had been really sick—that she had missed some days at work and had been fired.

Q: What else did you talk about?

A: I asked her who the guy was in her apartment. She told me her boyfriend, Roy, had moved in with her to help pay expenses. She said the beer in the refrigerator was his. I reminded Sherry that I had told her not to associate with Roy since he is currently on probation for DUI.

Q: What else?

A: I asked to see Sherry's AA/NA card. Once she handed it to me, I could see that she hadn't been to a meeting for over two weeks.

Q: Then what?

A: I told Sherry that I was going to have to report these violations to the court. I then left.

Q: Do you feel you can continue to supervise Ms. Davenport on probation?

A: I don't know. It just doesn't seem Sherry is willing to accept responsibility. Something needs to happen.

ASSISTANT STATE'S ATTORNEY: Thank you. No further questions.

THE COURT: Counsel, you may cross-examine.

DEFENSE COUNSEL: Thank you Your Honor. I just have a couple of questions. Now, Sherry never admitted to you that she had been drinking alcohol, is that correct?

A: Sherry never admitted to drinking the beer, but the point is that she is not to even be in possession of any alcohol.

Q: Sherry never admitted to leaving the state, did she?

A: No, but I can put two and two together.

Q: What did you do after leaving Sherry's apartment that day?

A: I went back to my office and prepared a report of violation to send to the State's Attorney's Office.

Q: Anything else?

A: Yes. I contacted Roy's probation officer and informed him of what I had observed that day.

DEFENSE COUNSEL: Nothing else, Judge.

THE COURT: Does the prosecutor have anything further?

ASSISTANT STATE'S ATTORNEY: No. No other witnesses.

THE COURT: Does the defense wish to present evidence?

DEFENSE COUNSEL: We do not intend to call witnesses, Your Honor, but would like to provide the court with an explanation and a recommendation.

THE COURT: Very well counsel. Proceed.

DEFENSE COUNSEL: Sherry has been through some difficult times. As she told her probation officer, she was sick. She had a really bad cold and did not want to go to work or to her meetings for fear she would infect others. When she lost her job, Sherry allowed her boyfriend to move in with her, but only because she needed financial assistance in order to pay the rent and other expenses. By the weekend when Sherry was finally feeling better, she had the opportunity to go to Wisconsin with a friend. She would have asked for permission to go, but it was the weekend and she couldn't contact her probation officer. Sherry intended to be back in time for her appointment with her PO but her friend's car broke down while they were in The Dells. Sherry would have called her probation officer but the battery died on her cell phone and she didn't have her charger. So you see, Your Honor, Sherry fully intended to comply with the conditions of her probation. After the probation officer left Sherry's apartment that day, Roy's probation officer showed up. Roy is now serving time in the Columbia County Jail so is no longer living with Sherry.

Your Honor, Sherry would like another chance. She wants to prove to the court, and to her probation officer, that she can comply with the conditions of her probation. On behalf of my client, I ask that the court continue Sherry on probation without any additional restrictions. I would hate to see this young woman's probation revoked and a prison sentence imposed. Since Sherry is currently looking for a job, I ask that she not be sentenced to jail time either. A jail sentence would simply exacerbate her problems.

THE COURT: What is the position of the prosecutor?

ASSISTANT STATE'S ATTORNEY: We ask that the court find the defendant in violation of her probation as alleged in the Petition. We ask the court to revoke her probation and resentence the defendant on the underlying theft charge for which she was placed on probation. The excuses offered by the defendant today are no better than the excuses she gave the court at the time of her sentencing. The court previously informed the defendant that probation is a privilege. She has abused that privilege and now it should be taken away. The defendant's probation officer has a heavy caseload. The defendant appears incapable of successfully completing probation. She is simply wasting valuable resources. We recommend the defendant be sent to prison. Thank you.

THE COURT: I will now issue my decision on probation conditions 3, 5, 6, 8, 11 and 12.

PROBATION REVOCATION EXERCISE

NAME ____

COURSE ____

DATE ____

Please provide full and complete responses to the following five questions.

1. Does it appear the judge complied with the requirements of Supreme Court Rule 402A before asking Davenport to admit or deny the allegations in the Petition? Referring to the transcript from that hearing, what supports your answer?

2. While the probation officer was testifying, the defense attorney objected three times on the basis of hearsay. The judge sustained the first two objections, but overruled the third. Why? Explain.

3. Did the probation officer violate any of Sherry's constitutional rights by looking around her apartment on the day of the home visit? Explain.

4. If you were the Judge in the Davenport case, would you find Sherry violated conditions: 3, 5, 6, 8, 11 and/or 12? Explain your reasoning for each allegation.

5. If you were the Judge, would you follow the recommendation of Sherry's attorney or the prosecutor? Would you order something other than what was recommended? Explain.

APPENDIX

COLUMBIA CITY POLICE
ARREST REPORT

Case No.____________________ **Arrest Date**________________

Name of person arrested: (enter on line below) Alias:

____

Address of suspect: City: State:

____

SSN: Age: Race: Sex: Eyes: Hair:

____

Ht. Wt. DOB: Place of Birth:

____

Location of arrest: Time of arrest:

____

Where offense committed: Date: Time:

____

Circle all that apply:
Armed: No Yes-weapon ________________________ Drunk Drinking Resisted Cursed

Vehicle Involved:
Year _____ Make ______ Model ______ Color _____ License #______________ State _________

Name of Complainant: DOB: Relationship (if any)

____

Address of Complainant: Home phone:

____

City, State: Work phone:

____

Name and address of witness(es):

____
____
____

Offense(s) suspected or charged: Statute:

____
____
____

Arresting officer(s): ____

Report made by: ____

Columbia City Police—Arrest Report **Page 2**

Photos taken? No:_____ Yes,
by:____

Prints lifted? No:_____ Yes,
by:____

Vehicle Information: [Include Year, Make, Model, Color, VIN, Plate, State]

____

Property Information: Stolen:_____ Recovered:_____ Damaged:_____

____

Narrative: [Use additional sheets if necessary]

COLUMBIA CITY POLICE DEPARTMENT
MIRANDA RIGHTS WAIVER FORM

Name: ____

SSN: ______________________________ DOB: ___________________________

Date: ______________________________ Time: ___________________________

Location: ____

On this date and at the time and location noted above, I met with Officer__________________

______________________________________, with the Columbia Police Department.

Before I was asked any questions to which the answers could be incriminating, I was advised of the following and was afforded an opportunity to ask questions if I had any:

1. I have the right to remain silent. Initials: _____

2. Anything I say or do may be used against me in a court of law. Initials: _____

3. I have the right to speak with a lawyer before questioning begins. If I cannot afford a lawyer, one will be appointed for me at no personal expense. Initials: _____

4. I have the right to stop answering questions at any time. Initials: _____

5. I wish to waive my right to a lawyer and speak with the officer. Initials: _____

Signature of Interviewee:____

Signature of Officer:____

Signature of Witness:____

Statute
CRIME VICTIMS
725 ILCS 120/4 RIGHTS OF CRIME VICTIMS

(a) Crime victims shall have the following rights:

1. The right to be treated with fairness and respect for their dignity and privacy throughout the criminal justice process.
2. The right to notification of court proceedings.
3. The right to communicate with the prosecution.
4. The right to make a statement to the court at sentencing.
5. The right to information about the conviction, sentence, imprisonment, and release of the accused.
6. The right to the timely disposition of the case following the arrest of the accused.
7. The right to be reasonably protected from the accused through the criminal justice process.
8. The right to be present at the trial and all other court proceedings on the same basis as the accused, unless the victim is to testify and the court determines that the victim's testimony would be materially affected if the victim hears other testimony at the trial.
9. The right to have present at all court proceedings, including proceedings under the Juvenile Court Act of 1987 [705 ILCS 405/1-1 et seq.], subject to the admonition of the rules of confidentiality and subject to the rules of evidence, a victim-witness specialist, an advocate, or other support person of the victim's choice.
10. The right to restitution.

(b) A statement and explanation of the rights of crime victims set forth in paragraph (a) of this Section shall be given to a crime victim at the initial contact with the criminal justice system by the appropriate authorities and shall be conspicuously posted in all court facilities.

Index

www.ingramcontent.com/pod-product-compliance
Ingram Content Group UK Ltd.
Pitfield, Milton Keynes, MK11 3LW, UK
UKHW051508290926
15471UKWH00008B/1497

9 781465 220820